WHAT YOUR COLLEAGUES ARE

"The authors have done an amazing job of outlining the importance of building a sense of belonging for all stakeholders in education. The focus is on building positive relationships where everyone feels welcomed, invited, present, known, accepted, involved, heard, supported, befriended, needed, and loved. This is the core of what all educators need to invest their time and energy in. Once you create this sense of belonging, you can then tap into each student and educator's true potential. The sky's the limit once you make this happen."

Dick Keeler
Principal at Central Valley Academy

"*Belonging in School* is a delightful primer on how schools can make students, staff, parents and guardians, and community members feel welcome. Students work for people they like in places they like. This book provides a pathway to create those conditions and ensure inclusivity, connectedness, and academic success for all."

Zac Robbins
Superintendent
Marysville School District

"Yessss! (Or maybe—Finally!) A whole book devoted to building the kind of culture in schools that's worth restoring. Every kid desires and deserves to belong. Teachers, listen up! Content knowledge matters less if you don't know how to build community. The authors break down the dimensions of belonging in a way that engages educators and shows them how to create and hold space for every student."

Shawn Bush
Director of Student Services
Metropolitan School District of Lawrence Township

"Dr. Smith's work with our districts has been nothing short of transformative. With a deep understanding of the critical importance of creating an inclusive, supportive school environment, Dr. Smith has guided our educators and administrators to rethink traditional disciplinary approaches. Instead of punitive measures, we now focus on restorative practices, conflict resolution, and social-emotional learning. The result has been a marked decrease in disciplinary incidents and a notable increase in student engagement and satisfaction.

Belonging in School takes us to the next level in our journey toward creating a more inclusive, supportive, and positive educational environment. The illustrated playbook is a comprehensive guide that offers practical, actionable strategies for fostering belonging not only among students but also among teachers and staff. This holistic approach recognizes that when educators and staff feel a sense of belonging, it naturally extends to students, creating a ripple effect of positivity and engagement throughout our schools."

Summer Prather-Smith
Director of Engagement and School Climate
Santa Rita Union School District

BELONGING in SCHOOL

BELONGING in SCHOOL

An Illustrated Playbook

CREATING A PLACE WHERE KIDS WANT TO **LEARN** & TEACHERS WANT TO **STAY**

DOMINIQUE SMITH · DOUGLAS FISHER · NANCY FREY
VINCENT POMPEI · RACHAEL STEWART
ILLUSTRATED BY TARYL HANSEN

CORWIN
Fisher & Frey

FOR INFORMATION:

Corwin
A SAGE Company
2455 Teller Road
Thousand Oaks, California 91320
(800) 233-9936
www.corwin.com

SAGE Publications Ltd.
1 Oliver's Yard
55 City Road
London EC1Y 1SP
United Kingdom

SAGE Publications India Pvt. Ltd.
Unit No 323-333, Third Floor, F-Block
International Trade Tower Nehru Place
New Delhi 110 019
India

SAGE Publications Asia-Pacific Pte. Ltd.
18 Cross Street #10-10/11/12
China Square Central
Singapore 048423

Vice President and
 Editorial Director: Monica Eckman
Director and Publisher: Lisa Luedeke
Associate Content
 Development Editor: Sarah Ross
Editorial Assistant: Zachary Vann
Production Editor: Tori Mirsadjadi
Copy Editor: Heather Kerrigan
Typesetter: C&M Digitals (P) Ltd.
Proofreader: Barbara Coster
Indexer: Integra
Illustrator: Taryl Hansen
Cover Designer: Gail Buschman
Marketing Manager: Megan Naidl

Printed in the United States of America

Library of Congress Cataloging-in-Publication Data

Names: Smith, Dominique, author. | Frey, Nancy, 1959- author. | Fisher, Douglas, 1965- author. | Stewart, Rachael (Career programs director), author. | Pompei, Vincent, author.

Title: Belonging in school : creating a place where kids want to learn and teachers want to stay : illustrated playbook/Dominique Smith, Nancy Frey, Douglas Fisher, Rachael Stewart, Vincent Pompei.

Description: Thousand Oaks, California : Corwin, [2024] | Includes bibliographical references and index.

Identifiers: LCCN 2023057355 | ISBN 9781071936030 (spiral bound) | ISBN 9781071946732 (epub) | ISBN 9781071946749 (epub) | ISBN 9781071946756 (pdf)

Subjects: LCSH: Students—Psychology. | Belonging (Social psychology) | Teachers—Job satisfaction. | Classroom environment.

Classification: LCC LB1117 .S558 2024 | DDC 371.102/2—dc23/eng/20240104
LC record available at https://lccn.loc.gov/2023057355

This book is printed on acid-free paper.

24 25 26 27 28 10 9 8 7 6 5 4 3

CONTENTS

Visit the companion website at
resources.corwin.com/belongingplaybook
for downloadable resources.

PUBLISHER'S ACKNOWLEDGMENTS

Corwin gratefully acknowledges the contributions of the following reviewers:

Helene Alalouf
Education Consultant/Instructional Coach
New York, NY

Alisa Barrett
Director of Instruction
Greenfield, OH

Melissa Black
Elementary Teacher and Education Consultant
Washington, DC

Ti'Gre McNear
Learning and Development Consultant
Carmel, IN

Andy Shoenborn
High School English Teacher
Midland, MI

ABOUT THE AUTHORS

Dominique Smith, **EdD**, is a principal, social worker, teacher, and mentor. Smith earned his master's degree in social work from the University of Southern California and his doctorate in educational leadership at San Diego State University. He is passionate about creating school cultures that honor student voice and build student and educator confidence and competence. Dr. Smith is a national trainer in restorative practices, classroom management, belonging, leadership, and the culture of achievement. He is the winner of the National School Safety Award from the School Safety Advocacy Council and the coauthor of *The Restorative Practices Playbook, The Social and Emotional Learning Playbook, Leader Credibility,* and *How Leadership Works*. As a current school principal, Dr. Smith works to ensure that all students know that they belong and that they are provide the supports necessary to achieve success.

Douglas Fisher is professor and chair of educational leadership at San Diego State University and a teacher leader at Health Sciences High and Middle College. Previously, Fisher was an early intervention teacher and elementary school educator. He is the recipient of an International Reading Association William S. Grey citation of merit and an Exemplary Leader award from the Conference on English Leadership of NCTE, as well as a Christa McAuliffe award for excellence in teacher education. In 2022, he was inducted into the Reading Hall of Fame by the Literacy Research Association. He has published numerous articles on reading and literacy, differentiated instruction, and curriculum design, as well as books such as *PLC+; Visible Learning for*

Literacy; *Comprehension: The Skill, Will, and Thrill of Reading*; *How Feedback Works*; *Teaching Reading*; and most recently, *Teaching Students to Drive Their Learning*. Fisher loves being an educator and hopes to share that passion with others.

Nancy Frey is a professor in educational leadership at San Diego State University and a teacher leader at Health Sciences High and Middle College. She is a member of the International Literacy Association's Literacy Research Panel. Her published titles include *Visible Learning in Literacy, This Is Balanced Literacy, Removing Labels, Rebound, The Social-Emotional Learning Playbook, and How Scaffolding Works*. Frey is a credentialed special educator, reading specialist, and administrator in California and learns from teachers and students every day.

Vincent Pompei, EdD, is an assistant professor in educational leadership at San Diego State University. Prior to joining the university, he spent nearly a decade as the National Director of Youth Well-Being Programming at the Human Rights Campaign, the nation's largest civil rights organization dedicated to LGBTQ+ equality. His research interests include student mental wellness, identity-safe schools, culturally responsive pedagogy, and LGBTQ+ inclusion. Pompei was acknowledged by the National Education Association as a Classroom Superhero and was honored by the *Advocate Magazine*, Equality California, and the California PTA for his dedication to creating safe and inclusive schools.

Rachael Stewart, EdD, holds the position of professor and director of academic and career programs within the Division of Student Affairs and Campus Diversity at San Diego State University. Her area of expertise lies in the study of organizational leadership, change, policy, and practices in education systems. Her research is primarily focused on the creation of conducive environments for student success through engagement, retention, and post-graduate outcomes.

Taryl Hansen, is a National Board Certified Teacher, Associate Trainer of Cognitive Coaching SM, a highly skilled visual practitioner, and the founder of Frame the Message Ink. As a live graphic recorder, Taryl works internationally to create vibrant and engaging visuals that bring essential elements to the forefront for learners, enhancing retention, engagement, and inspiring learners to collaborate in more meaningful ways.

"THE SECRET, ALICE, IS TO SURROUND YOURSELF WITH PEOPLE WHO MAKE YOUR HEART SMILE. IT'S THEN, AND ONLY THEN, THAT YOU'LL FIND WONDERLAND."
Often attributed to Lewis Carroll

INTRODUCTION

What does it mean to have a sense of belonging? Belonging is a visceral feeling: You know when you feel it—and you *really* know when you don't. But what does belonging actually entail? "Belonging is the feeling that we're part of a larger group that values, respects, and cares for us—and to which we feel we have something to contribute."[1] Let's take that definition apart.

- *Feeling:* It's emotional and psychological, and we experience it.
- *Larger group:* It's about membership with other people.
- *Values:* There is a sense of worth or importance.
- *Respects:* There is admiration for the qualities each person has.
- *Cares:* There is concern and attention.
- *Something to contribute:* The group benefits from each person's contributions.

Students with a strong sense of belonging in a classroom perform better academically.[2] When students don't feel that they belong, their performance suffers. This is not just some fluffy mumble jumble: There is a strong research base that supports the need for schools to create systems that foster student belonging. In fact, several meta-analyses point to the fact that belonging keeps us learning. The effect size for belonging is 0.46, just above average of all the things that we do in school to ensure learning.[3]

Figure I.1 • Effect Size for Belonging

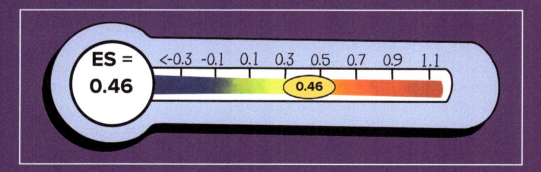

Belonging is a key factor that allows other influences to take hold. Belonging serves as a gatekeeper for all the other aspects of learning to take root. If students do not feel that they belong in a class, then it is unlikely that the amazing instruction being provided to them will significantly improve their learning. Instead, students with a low sense of belonging spend time questioning their status and membership in the group and fail to achieve at high levels. For them, the gate is closed, and they are on the outside of learning, looking in.

The impact of belonging also extends far beyond academics. Studies suggest that belonging also affects our health and well-being.[4] Not only do students learn more when they feel that they belong, but they also experience positive health outcomes, including self-reports of wellness and reduced number of doctor visits.[5]

The reverse is also true, and a diminished sense of belonging can break along racial, ethnic, and ability lines. Black adolescent students are at higher risk for reporting a lack of belonging and school connectedness.[6] Another study showed that there was a relationship between sense of belonging and suicide ideation and attempts for Black students, with the risk increasing by 35 percent when students did not feel that they belonged.[7] Another study found that belonging at school reduced suicide ideation among Latino/x/e students.[8] Similarly, a study of students with learning disabilities found that higher levels of school and family connectedness were linked to reduced emotional distress, suicide attempts, and involvement in violence.[9]

Importantly, students can have a stronger sense of belonging in one class or grade and a diminished sense of belonging in another class or grade. For all of us, belonging is malleable, and it changes based on the experiences we are currently having or have had in the past. Teachers and leaders can design environments and experiences to create situations in which belonging is fostered—and this is an essential commitment for educators to make. If we neglect the environment and fail to ensure that all students feel that they belong, our disregard diminishes our teaching and our students' learning.

HOW TO USE THIS BOOK

We have organized this playbook to support the important conversations caring educators have about how classrooms and schools can ensure that every child feels a sense of belonging and connectedness to their school. Module 1 provides an overview of the eleven dimensions of belonging that follow in Modules 2–12. We suggest you begin with Module 1 to build foundational knowledge. After that, please dive into the modules in any order that aligns with your purposes. The dimensions of belonging inform one another, but they are in no way meant to suggest a hierarchy, chronological importance, or order of operations.

You'll find that every module features three evidence-based actions that teachers can apply to create the kinds of classrooms and schools that invest in every student's sense of belonging. Some of the actions may resonate with you more than others. We have tried to balance actions that are useful at the elementary and secondary levels.

Given that this is a playbook, you'll notice several interactive features:

- An **Essential Question** frames each module and is intended to build schema.

- **Two Truths and a Lie** near the beginning of the module allows you to consider several statements and then determine which ones are supported by the research and which one captures a common misconception. We invite you to return to these after reading the module to see if your thinking has been validated or extended.

- A **Quick Start** follows each profiled action, allowing you an opportunity to reflect on the content presented and prioritize the actions you can begin, as well as resources you may need to do so.

- The **Case in Point** in each module offers a scenario and an opportunity to see educators working together to resolve a dilemma. We've also included a **What's Your Advice?** feature, which allows you to make recommendations based on what you have learned and experienced.

- **What's Next?** appears at the end of every module and invites you to reflect on your learning and take actions of your own: What will you start, stop, and continue? It allows you space to scale your level of understanding so that you can keep learning after finishing the module.

Again, this playbook is meant to engage *you*. Please mark it up and complete the various tasks. The narrative in each module provides current and tested research as well as informed recommendations for practice. Your willingness to engage in the exercises in this playbook demonstrates your commitment to your students. Happy reading.

OVERVIEW: DIMENSIONS OF BELONGING

Most of us have had an experience when we did not feel that we belonged. Maybe it was in school, but maybe it was in our personal life. When we had that feeling, most likely we did not perform well, and we may even have tried to escape from the situation. The same is true for our students. When they don't feel they belong, they may try to escape from or avoid situations that are uncomfortable. Or they may choose not to be present at all. If we really do care about their learning and we want to live up to our mission and vision of schools, then we need to implement practices that increase students' sense of belonging. To learn best, students need to feel all these dimensions.[1]

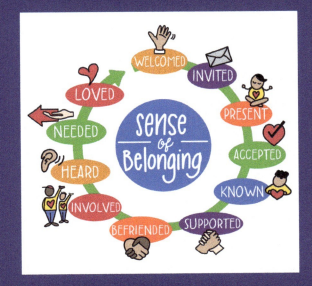

For now, we'll ask that you consider each dimension, how you would define it, and what actions you might take to address it. In the modules that follow, we'll provide an essential question for each dimension, definitions and parameters, actions that can foster belonging for each dimension, and indicators of success. For now, familiarize yourself with the dimensions and activate your background knowledge.

Consider the following quote: "We all hope that students will feel truly 'at home' in their classrooms. We want them to feel valued and accepted by their peers and teachers. We strive to create connections among students that lead to reciprocal relationships."[2] If you share that vision, this playbook is for you.

Essential Question:

HOW CAN WE LAY A SUCCESSFUL FOUNDATION TO BUILD STUDENTS' SENSE OF BELONGING?

TWO TRUTHS AND A LIE

Two of these statements are true; one is false. Can you spot the lie?

1. A low sense of belonging is associated with physical health concerns, including decreased immune function, a decline in cardiovascular health, and higher levels of cortisol, a hormone associated with distress.

2. A student's sense of belonging in school extends far beyond their academic years and impacts their sense of wellness into adulthood.

3. A person who possesses identities that are valued by their community will have a permanent sense of belonging.

A sense of belonging is crucial for well-being, and it is rooted in our deepest needs as humans to connect with others. Consider the toll the isolation during the COVID-19 pandemic took on so many people—perhaps you too. Isolation and diminished belongingness are well-documented threats to the physical and mental well-being of people across the lifespan.[3]

The sense of belonging students experience in school can persist into adulthood. People with a higher sense of belonging are more likely to achieve at higher rates, setting into motion an increased likelihood of being able to reach their aspirations as adults.[4] While it's by no means a guarantee, those who experience belongingness in school set a pattern for seeking belongingness as adults.[5]

The lie? A person's identities are not the golden ticket to belonging.[6] Too often, a person's sense of belonging is contingent on performance, not on their value as a person. As one example, think of the school athlete who has a bad game. Suddenly, their identity no longer affords them the sense of belonging they possessed days earlier.

SCHOOL CONDITIONS THAT IMPACT BELONGING

There are literally thousands of articles about the value and impact of belonging in schools. As we noted in the introduction, the impact of a sense of belonging on academic achievement is strong. In other words, one of the influences on whether or not students learn is their belief that they belong in the classroom and school. Belongingness is more than mere affiliation. Belongingness is marked by relationships that are lasting and meaningful.[7]

One question concerns the conditions that influence students' sense of belonging. What are the various school factors that foster—or hamper—students' beliefs that they belong? One way to answer this question is to look at correlations between different factors and then test to see how powerful each of these is in explaining the outcome. The result shows paths of relationships between conditions, called a path analysis. In this kind of study, the relations are linear and additive, and the causal flow is in one direction. Note the direction of the arrows and where there are arrows to determine whether there is a relationship between two conditions.

This path analysis is from an investigation of students' sense of school belonging.[8]

Figure O.1 • Path Analysis of Student Sense of Belonging

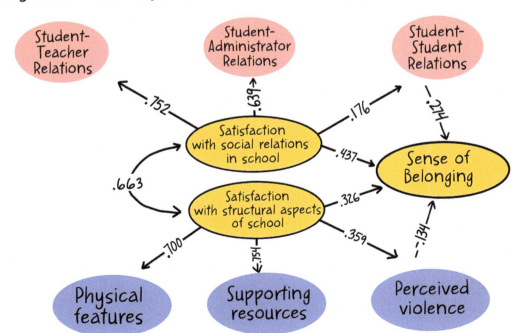

Let's start in the middle. Note that students' satisfaction with the social relations in the school is correlated with their satisfaction with the structural aspects of the school. The correlation is 0.663, which is strong and suggests that these two concepts are related. As the image displays, each of these factors relates to an overall sense of belonging. The correlation between the social relations and belonging is 0.437 and the structural aspects and belonging is 0.326. Together, these correlations add up to 0.763, which implies that these two constructs explain a significant amount of the variance in students' sense of belonging. We'll focus on the structural aspects of school first. We'll turn our attention to social relations in the next section.

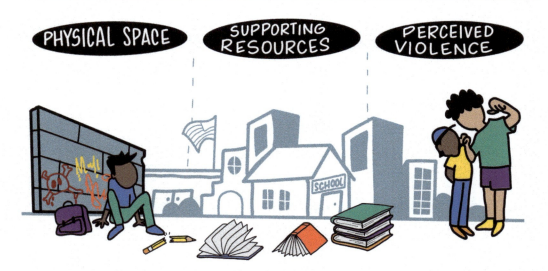

Three factors contribute to the overall satisfaction with the structural aspects of the school: the physical features, supporting resources, and perceptions of violence.

The *physical features* are an important factor. There is a strong correlation between physical features and satisfaction with the structural aspects, at 0.700. Physical features are the directly observable aspects of the building, which include lighting, noise, architecture, interior design, furniture, and other indoor and outdoor facilities.[9] Some schools are cleaner than others; some have graffiti that's not quickly removed. Some schools have specialized environments (arts, physical education, and video production to name a few) and others do not. At the classroom level, the physical features include room arrangement, accessibility, seating, the use of wall space (such as bulletin boards and displays), and physical climate.

Figure O.2 • Effect Size for School Size

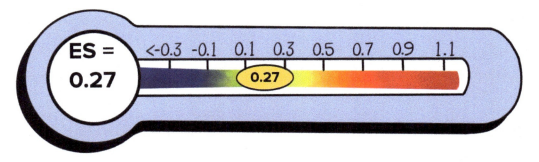

In addition, school size is one of the physical features that contributes to students' perceptions of the structure, with larger schools receiving less support. The effect size for school size on learning is 0.27, which is not a major influence but one that is contributing to the overall success of some students.

A second factor is *supporting resources*. The correlation between supporting resources and satisfaction with the structural aspects is also high: 0.754. This includes instructional materials, such as books and supplies. Do students have to share materials, or are there sufficient materials for students to complete learning tasks with their own supplies? Other supporting resources are for out-of-class activities, including field trips, musical instruments, or sports equipment. In schools where students recognize they have appropriate resources, satisfaction increases.

The third element in this path analysis is *perceived violence*. The correlation between perceived violence and satisfaction with the structural aspects is negative: −0.359. When students *perceive* the school to be unsafe, their satisfaction is reduced, and it has a negative impact on their sense of belonging (−0.134). Safety is an important concern of students, and it includes knowing that their belongings are safe in their classrooms. All students need spaces they can call their own to store their personal materials and supplies.

Perceptions of violence are influenced by bullying and cyberbullying, which have been documented to compromise students' sense of belonging.[10] The effect size of bullying is −0.32, a negative impact on learning. Even witnesses to bullying suffer a reduced sense of belonging, especially when the bullying is not addressed by staff.[11] Further, students may perceive verbal, psychological, or physical violence from teachers to students, students to students, and between adults on campus. This factor includes not only personal experiences of violence, but also a general sense of safety on the campus.

TAKE ACTION

Prioritize a safe and secure school climate. We recognize that this first action step involves a wider web of professionals and community members; however, it is a crucial factor for promoting belonging. The conversations about school structures and accessibility can result in vital actions that the adults in the school can collaboratively enact. SchoolSafety.gov is an interagency effort to promote schools that are physically secure and emotionally and psychologically safe. Explore their offerings to support schools to enhance their programs and activities. Resources include those for supporting student mental wellness, stopping and preventing bullying, and improving school climate.[12]

QUICK START

	I can start this tomorrow!	I can begin this month	I need to discuss this with others	Resources needed
Inventory the supplies and materials your students use regularly in your classroom, and request new supplies as needed.				
Set up a weekly or daily classroom clean-up schedule with your students to maintain an orderly environment.				
Develop and implement a safety plan that includes actions the school can take to prevent bullying behavior and address bullying behavior.				

SOCIAL RELATIONS IN THE SCHOOL

In the previous section, we examined the ways the structural aspects of a school contribute to students' sense of school belonging. In this section, let's turn our attention to the social relations in school and the role this component plays in school belonging.

Three factors contribute to students' satisfaction with the social relations in the school. The first is *student-teacher relations*. The correlation between student-teacher relations and overall satisfaction with the social relationships in school is 0.752—again very powerful. The effect size of student-teacher relationships is 0.62, indicating that this has an influence on students' learning. Students want teachers to be fair, to respect and honor them, and to care about them as individuals.

The second contribution to students' satisfaction with social relations is *student-administrator relations*. The correlation between student-administrator relations and overall satisfaction with the social relationships in school is 0.639—again very powerful, but a bit of a surprise. There is ample research about student-teacher relationships, but more limited evidence about the role that school leaders play in creating a sense of belonging. These data reinforce the idea that leaders are primarily responsible for creating and maintaining the climate of the school, which has an effect size of 0.49. It also indicates that the leaders' social interactions with the students influenced the students' satisfaction with the social relations in their school.

Interestingly, there is evidence that school leaders are more influential than teachers on students' school engagement,[13] which includes participation in school-related activities, achievement of high grades, amount of time spent on homework, and rate of homework completion—as well as delinquency, truancy, or misbehavior. Importantly, teachers have a stronger influence on student engagement in learning, which has been defined as "the degree of attention, curiosity, interest, optimism, and passion that students show when they are learning or being taught, which extends to the level of motivation they have to learn and progress in their education."[14]

The correlation between *student-student relations* and overall satisfaction with the social relationships in school is 0.176, which is relatively low. However, this factor also has a direct relationship to belonging, independent of the overall satisfaction students feel with social relationships, with a correlation of 0.274. It seems that when it comes to belonging, students rely more on the adults in the school to establish the conditions for social relations. When the social relations between students and teachers and students and administrators are accounted for, the role of peers is reduced. It's also important to note that friendship has an effect size of 0.38, meaning that having friends facilitates learning.

TAKE ACTION

Prioritize student-teacher relationships. The fact that you are reading this playbook says a lot about how valuable positive student-teacher relationships are to you. However, although you probably invest a lot of time at the beginning of the school year for getting-to-know-you activities, it is crucial to understand that relationships require steady, consistent, and long-term investment. Devote the same kind of energy you put into academic planning by augmenting it with relationship planning. Have at least one activity every week that is expressly designed to build relationships with your class.

Involve families in your efforts from the beginning. Families and guardians are the keepers of the child's history, and they know what works and what doesn't. Develop relationships with students' families/guardians so they understand they are a part of a team. Regular communication is incredibly valuable. If you're an elementary teacher, you might send out a weekly newsletter. As a secondary teacher, you might use a classroom blog or a weekly automated message service to inform families of what their young person is learning about. These communications don't need to be long and involved. A few sentences each week can help you become a presence in the lives of families, even though you may rarely share the same physical space.

QUICK START

	I can start this tomorrow!	I can begin this month	I need to discuss this with others	Resources needed
Make a point of laughing with students, smiling, and taking pleasure in their company.				
Make time for regular one-to-one communication with each student.				
Make sure your positive communications with families about the student outnumber negative ones.				

KNOWING IF STUDENTS FEEL THEY BELONG

There are several extensive surveys to determine the level of belonging that students feel in their school. However, most educators are not investigating belonging as a researcher. Thankfully, there are tools that teachers can use more quickly. These tools have strong psychometric properties, which also allows educators to avoid making decisions based on faulty information.[15] For example, the following five questions used on the Trends in International Mathematics and Science Study (TIMSS) provide a quick way that teachers can gauge the level of belonging perceived by their students:[16]

- I like being in school.
- I feel safe when I am at school.
- I feel like I belong at this school.
- Teachers at my school are fair to me.
- I am proud to go to this school.

The survey asks students to respond to each statement with a number: (4) agree a lot, (3) agree a little, (2) disagree a little, or (1) disagree a lot.

The Center for Whole-Child Education at Arizona State University offers two free tools and guidance for setting up a Google Form so that schools can track students' well-being weekly or monthly. The questionnaire for grades 3–5 consists of six questions (e.g., "I've been feeling cared about by others"), while the version for grades 6–12 has twelve items (e.g., "I've been feeling heard by others"). Educators can use their Well-Being Index to create individual and class reports and to visualize data so that adults can respond. In their study of the instrument, secondary students remarked that the use of the tool could prompt peers to engage in self-reflection "without a lot of pressure."[17] An advantage of regularly using simple surveys like the TIMSS scale or the Well-Being Index is that it provides educators with ways to regularly gauge and respond to the contexts that influence well-being.

TAKE ACTION

Understand belonging data in context. Data collection on sense of belonging is a snapshot in time, and it is influenced by other variables, such as friendships and events that occur in students' personal lives. The power of such data lies in repeated measures so that you can identify trends and patterns. For instance, are there certain times of the school year when a sense of belonging tends to wax or wane?

Normalize belongingness. A sense of belonging doesn't remain fixed and static. Like other human emotions, we all experience varying degrees of belongingness. It is important for students to understand that when a person doesn't feel like they belong, it doesn't mean there is something wrong with *them*. Rather, it may be the situation and conditions that need to be crafted. Emphasize that talking about feeling like you don't belong is a healthy response that can spark help.

Make predictions about your students' perceptions of belonging. Choose a student whom you know well. Predict how that student would respond to each of the questions using the TIMSS scale (Table O.1). Then predict how the average student in your grade or department would respond. Finally, predict how the average student in your school would respond. This gives you the opportunity to consider the perspective of a variety of students.

Table O.1 • The TMSS Scale

Item	Response from a student you know well: (4) agree a lot, (3) agree a little, (2) disagree a little, or (1) disagree a lot	Response from the average student in your grade or department: (4) agree a lot, (3) agree a little, (2) disagree a little, or (1) disagree a lot	Response from the average student in your school: (4) agree a lot, (3) agree a little, (2) disagree a little, or (1) disagree a lot	Reflections on the data
I like being in school.				
I feel safe when I am at school.				
I feel like I belong at this school.				
Teachers at my school are fair to me.				
I am proud to go to this school.				

Our perceptions about how a student feels may be different from the actual perception of the student. For example, a quiet student who often smiles when you look at them could be dealing with significant challenges with bullying or in their home life.

QUICK START

	I can start this tomorrow!	I can begin this month	I need to discuss this with others	Resources needed
Find out whether your school collects student-belonging data through climate surveys or other instruments.				
Talk about belonging with your students in the context of academic learning, such as making connections to fictional characters or historical figures.				
Don't forget families! Survey them to find out what they want and need.				

CASE IN POINT: HEAT MAP FOR BULLYING

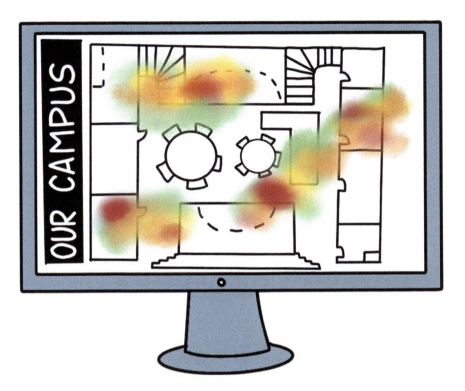

Azura High School's wellness committee is a student-driven effort of the Associated Student Body. Members include learners in student government groups and adult advisers. The creation of the wellness committee was inspired by the work of Not in Our Schools (NIOS), a national organization committed to eliminating hate crimes and bullying in schools.

To identify and understand concerns about student belonging, the wellness committee decided to use a heat map process developed by NIOS. They surveyed students at each grade level, asking them to indicate on a digital map of the layout of the school any spots in the school where they had witnessed, participated in, or been the victim of verbal or physical harassment in the current school year. Each such spot was marked by students with a digital X. Responses were anonymous but reported by grade levels.

The student group viewed the results of the survey and developed a heat map of the "hot spots" where events like this were most likely to occur. The wellness committee was surprised to learn that certain hallways and stairwells were identified more often. The orchestra room was singled out, which some members had not expected. Participating students also identified the cafeteria as a hot spot.

What's Your Advice?

- What recommendations would you make to the wellness committee about taking actions on their findings?

- Who are key stakeholders they should involve?

- What proactive actions would you recommend they take, beyond increased surveillance and adult presence?

ESSENTIAL QUESTION

How can we lay a successful foundation to build students' sense of belonging?

THINK ABOUT

- How do school structural conditions impact belonging?

- How do social relations impact belonging?

- How can you gauge and track school belonging with your own students?

START – STOP – KEEP

Based on what you learned in this module, answer the questions that follow.

Start: What practice(s) would you like to start doing?

Stop: What practice(s) would you like to stop doing?

Keep: What practice(s) would you like to keep doing?

NOTES

1 WELCOMED

Classrooms and schools have a feel to them, which is known as the climate of the organization. And the climate contributes to student learning. Interestingly, the effect size for the classroom climate is 0.26, meaning that it exerts a small but positive influence on learning. However, the school climate is more powerful, with an effect size of 0.49. This may be because students and staff experience the whole organization, including hallways, lunchrooms, and other locations.

Part of the climate effect is how welcomed people feel within a given environment. When we feel welcomed, we are more likely to be relaxed and less concerned about whether people are questioning our presence. When we feel unwelcomed, our attention shifts to escaping the environment or figuring out how to survive the situation. Often, this feeling of welcomed relates to our identities.

There is a relationship between identity and belonging, but they are not the same thing. Identity is who we are. It's the story we tell ourselves about ourselves. And those stories are influenced by the interactions we have with other people. We are complex beings, and there are many dimensions to our identities. Some aspects include

- **Family Identity:** Parent, guardian, sibling, twin, nephew, grandparent, cousin, guardian, caregiver, chosen family, and other caring adults who help care for the student
- **Skills Identity:** Athlete, mathematician, artist, leader, listener, person with (dis)ability, or problem solver are just a few
- **Cultural Identity:** Nationality, ethnicity, race, sexual orientation, gender identity, religious beliefs, social class, geographic region, etc.
- **Social Identity:** Peer group, team, clique, gang, club, memberships, occupation, and other affiliations

We carry our identities into every environment, but we may feel a need to hide aspects of our identities, often to fit in, or due to safety concerns. In doing so, we feel less welcome because we aren't comfortable being ourselves. In those cases, we may have a fleeting sense of belonging, but it's likely that we continue to question our membership and value in the group. Making people feel welcomed in our classrooms and other school environments means that we recognize their many identities.

Essential Question:

HOW DOES THE ENVIRONMENT AND VARIOUS SITUATIONS CONVEY A CONSISTENT MESSAGE OF WELCOMING?

Indicators: Teachers described these indicators of a welcoming classroom and school environment. Use these indicators to assess your own environment.

Table 1.1 • What Being Welcomed Looks, Sounds, and Feels Like

What Does It Look Like?	What Does It Sound Like?	What Does It Feel Like?
• Showing genuine excitement • Arranging the physical environment to be clean and inviting • Knowing every student's name and greeting students • Ensuring that all students receive a welcome in a personal way • Sharing smiles, high-fives, hugs, etc. • Using materials and resources that reflect students' identities	• Greeting students personally • Pronouncing names correctly • Drawing students into conversation • Asking authentic questions • Noticing when students are absent and asking why • Showing enthusiasm for students' return or late arrival: "Welcome back! We missed your smile!" (or some other specific quality or trait) • Using inclusive and affirming language	• Authentic • Safe • Warm • Comfortable • Intentional • Genuine • Inclusive • Like home

TWO TRUTHS AND A LIE

Two of these statements are true; one is false. Can you spot the lie?

1. Families/caregivers who perceive a welcoming school environment have a heightened sense of responsibility to be involved, and they are more supportive of positive school behavior outside of school.

2. Greeting students at the door is a nice way to welcome them, but it doesn't impact learning.

3. The respectful and accurate use of students' names by teachers is associated with higher levels of student motivation, satisfaction, and engagement.

When we welcome students into the school and classroom, we are really extending a welcome to their entire family and caregivers. In fact, families/caregivers who don't feel welcomed in the school are less likely to participate in school functions, and they tend to make fewer supportive statements about the value of education and the school.[1] The school's ability to welcome families/caregivers requires knowing and understanding the community that it serves, which may not be the community that some of the educators live in or come from.

Notably, the people students live with vary widely and include grandparents, single-parent homes, LGBTQIA+ parents, blended families, and foster families. Additionally, the languages, cultures, ethnicities, and races of the people the school serves should be reflected throughout the building. For example, families/caregivers who communicate using different languages feel more welcome when translation services are proactive and readily available. Taking these factors into consideration conveys respect for the community.

The message of respect also extends to the students we serve, and it begins with acknowledgment. Make a point during the first week of school of using the names students go by, and use them often. Ask for help if you need guidance on pronunciation. Please don't give students a nickname or tell them their name is "too hard." Students identify their teachers' accurate and respectful use of their names as an affordance for building positive relationships. The accurate use of students' names boosts motivation, engagement, and school satisfaction.[2]

The lie, in this case, is that greetings at the door are nice but not impactful. Not only does this practice welcome students the moment they arrive at your door, but also it gives you visibility outside of your classroom to welcome other students passing by. There is good evidence that regular use of this practice increases student engagement and decreases disruptive behavior.[3] That's welcome news for us all!

GREETINGS

As simple as this may sound, we all like to be greeted when we enter a new environment. It's part of the social contract that humans have: We expect to be acknowledged. Greetings serve a basic communication function and increase the likelihood that the interaction will be positive. In fact, when students are greeted personally by their teacher before class, they engage in academic instruction and display on-task behavior more quickly than when they do not receive the same attention from their teacher.[4] Greeting students also fosters a safe and supportive environment for students from different cultures, who may face discrimination outside of school.[5] Greetings are especially important for transgender and gender-expansive students, because the recognition of their chosen name and pronouns is a key element in expressing support and acceptance of who they are.[6]

In one study of ten middle school classrooms, engagement increased by 20 percentage points and problematic behavior decreased by 9 percentage points when teachers started class by welcoming students at the door.[7] The intervention was simple. When greeting students at your door, include these steps:

- Say the student's name.

- Make eye contact and match it with a friendly facial expression. Note that in some cultures, eye contact can be considered disrespectful. When we truly know our students, and are culturally responsive, we will know which nonverbal messages work best for them.

- Use a friendly nonverbal greeting, such as a handshake, high-five, fist-bump, wave, or thumbs-up. Again, knowing our students and who appreciates physical contact is important.

- Give a few words of encouragement.

TAKE ACTION

Know names. Names are a significant part of our identity. Learn students' names, say them correctly, and use them often (and not as a correction for problematic behavior). If a name is unfamiliar for you, let the student know and ask them for help. Also, don't make up a nickname because you have a hard time pronouncing their name correctly. Keep practicing until you get it right.

Use context to support memory functions. Ask your students to write a short explanation of where their name came from or the meaning of one of their names (first, middle, last, chosen) so they can share it with the class. Model first: What is the story of your name? Encourage students to ask family/caregivers or use the internet to learn the historical meaning or origins of their name/s.

Monitor your nonverbal messages. When we're busy or stressed, our nonverbal behaviors don't always match our verbal behaviors. Students note the nonverbal behaviors, so they may still not feel welcomed if your nonverbal messages aren't friendly. Smile and make eye contact with each of them as they enter.

Avoid asking, "How are you?" Unless you have time to process the response, avoid using "How are you?" as a greeting. We have all learned that we're supposed to answer "fine" or "good," even when we might not be. Use other statements to greet students (e.g., "I'm happy you're here today!") and reserve "how are you" for times when you want to explore students' emotions.

Commit to hallways. Although it takes time away from other tasks, being present in the hallway regularly and greeting students is an investment in the smooth operation of the classroom. Work with your hallway colleagues so that you can take turns being in the hall at different times of the day. This ensures that the responsibility is shared and that teachers can count on times each day to take care of quick tasks. Make greeting students in the hall a habit rather than a random occurrence.

QUICK START

	I can start this tomorrow!	I can begin this month	I need to discuss this with others	Resources needed
Learn the names of every student in your class(es).				
Establish a greeting routine.				
Develop a daily rotating schedule with colleagues in your immediate area so that some teachers are present during each passing period.				

REPRESENTATION AS A TOOL FOR WELCOMING

Have you ever entered a room when there was a meeting, and you were not supposed to be there? Once you realized the error, you probably felt embarrassed and quickly turned on your heel to head the other way. Now imagine that as a lingering feeling some students experience every day, throughout the day. As humans, when we enter a new environment, we immediately take in the cues that let us know whether we belong. We look for visual signs that we are in the right place. We all need a sense of place to ground our daily selves.

The public spaces of the school should convey consistent messaging about the welcoming nature of the school. It seems obvious that welcome signs should be prominently displayed. But look closely to find signs that might otherwise counter this message. Those that say "No Students Allowed" or "Staff Only" undermine a message of welcome. It should be sufficient that confidential and private use areas are locked.

The walls of our classrooms also teach, and they can provide messages of welcome. Classrooms should spotlight people who have contributed to the subjects we teach, including those who may be less well known. They should also have ample room to display student-generated work that is representative of their identities. Too often, classrooms are filled to the brim with commercial products that limit the identities of the students within, and as a result, "children are muffled when what is displayed does not accurately reflect who they are in terms of gender, culture, and ethnicity."[8] Classrooms shouldn't look like a home design catalog filled with the latest trends. Such environments often reflect the aesthetic tastes of the teacher, with little space left for the learners within.

The physical space of the school and classroom extend to its accessibility. Thanks to the Americans with Disabilities Act, public buildings have become more accessible through things like Braille signage, ramps, and emergency systems that pair audible and visual alarms. However, it is easy to overlook the clutter that makes it difficult for someone who uses a wheelchair to navigate the classroom. People with larger bodies may struggle to find a chair that will accommodate their size because of armrests or because the classroom is filled with desks with attached seats. Keep in mind that it may not be a student who needs this accommodation; a family member/caregiver of a student or a colleague of yours may need it.

The way the information, policies, and expectations are written in a school's student handbook can also undermine a message of welcome. For example, dress code policies can target specific groups of students, such as banning certain hairstyles or hijabs, or by claiming that something is a "distraction" to other students. While dress codes should be in place to ensure health and safety, they should not be used to dictate appearance or communicate to the entire school community that certain people don't really belong. More school districts are simplifying their dress codes by stating gender-neutral requirements that don't single out groups (e.g., students are required to wear shirts, dresses, pants, and shoes that cover undergarments). As a classroom teacher, you may not be able to change unwelcoming language in your school's student handbook on your own, but you can bring it to the attention of your colleagues and administrators.

TAKE ACTION

Remove unwelcoming messages. Look for signage that counters welcoming messages in your classroom or school. Replace exclusionary messages that ban certain groups from specific locations, and develop signage that is respectful.

Take a visual inventory of hallways and classrooms. Identify positive messages about students, their families/caregivers, and the community. Each school should inspire a sense of place and respond to the ages of the students. The students in every school deserve to be educated in a place that reflects themselves and the world at large.

Clean up. Spaces that are messy and disorganized send a message to students that someone does not care enough. Take some time to organize and clean the classroom and leave specific instructions for janitors and maintenance staff about what needs to be done.

Analyze your school's current dress code policy. Are there rules that single out groups, such as the length of some students' hair? Are these associated with disciplinary actions (e.g., detention) or shaming techniques (e.g., dress code violation t-shirts)? If so, start the conversation about how these policies might be revised to promote a welcoming learning environment.

QUICK START

	I can start this tomorrow!	I can begin this month	I need to discuss this with others	Resources needed
Analyze the walls of your classroom for welcoming messages.				
Rearrange furniture as necessary for accessibility, collaboration, and community building.				
Conduct a visual inventory of the school with your team (e.g., community spaces, art/bulletin boards, signage, hallways).				

SITUATION CRAFTING

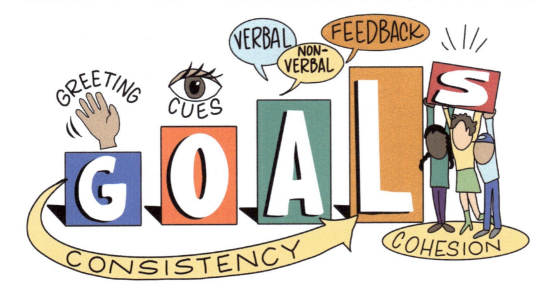

There is power in the situation itself. According to social psychologists, people's thoughts, actions, and emotions are influenced substantially by the social setting.[9] Situation crafting comes from the belonging research, and it takes the stance that rather than try to change people, we change the situations they're in. "Situation-crafting is all about molding situations in a way that helps people feel like they belong, and thus helps them to bring out their collective best."[10] In other words, it includes the intentional actions and plans we put in place to ensure that students feel welcomed.

Think of it this way—the aim is not to change students, but rather to change environments (situations) so that a deeper sense of student belonging is the outcome. It requires that we work so that situations are deliberately constructed to ensure that students consistently receive the three core messages of belonging:[11]

1. You are seen.

2. You have potential.

3. You are not alone.

For instance, being intentional about greeting students at the door is a form of situation crafting. Attending to the visual cues in a school to have messages that convey welcome is another example of situation crafting. Thus, each aspect of the situation (classroom or school) can be crafted to support students' belonging—or not.

Situation crafting can have powerful long-term effects. In one study, first-year college students met with graduating students who shared their stories of difficulties they faced three years earlier, pairing the stories with these messages: *It gets better, and you aren't alone in feeling the struggle. If you feel at times like you should quit and go home, that's a normal feeling and it will pass.* The researchers followed those first-year students for the next three years and found that all the participants, but especially students of color, benefited. They had higher grade-point averages and had fewer medical visits. These results indicated that this brief intervention had a "buffering effect against adversity."[12] This example shows what it looks like to successfully craft a situation that helps students understand their current situation in a different light.

An important aspect of situation crafting is recognizing that groups need to have goals that cannot be achieved individually. In fact, classroom cohesion is an accelerator of learning, with an effect size of 0.72. Classroom cohesion is the sense that the teacher and their students are working in harmony to achieve shared goals for learning. These goals, which are crafted such that students need each other to be successful, can include both academic and social aspects, such as these:

- We can support our peers when they feel frustrated as they learn new things.

- We can develop and explain the relationship between energy levels and the placement of the elements on the Periodic Table to our families/caregivers.

When students believe that these group goals apply to them, they begin to see the situation as supportive and welcoming. Situation crafting takes time, and one comment or action is unlikely to significantly alter students' thinking. But like water dripping on a rock, consistent implementation can create lasting change.

TAKE ACTION

Make strategic comments. A "just right" comment made at just the right time can alter students' perception of the situation. These comments should demonstrate confidence in the learner and leave them with something to think about. For example, you might say, "You are braver than you believe," "You can do hard things," or "How did you challenge yourself today?"

Tell stories. When you notice that a situation is particularly trying for a student, ask them if they want to hear a story. Stories help us make sense of situations yet keep us feeling safe because they are about others. You can tell a story from your personal life or another that helps the student think differently about the situation.

Provide empathetic feedback. Some students interpret teacher feedback as evidence that the teacher does not like them. As a result, they may feel that they aren't welcomed and don't belong. To help students begin to accept feedback more willingly, teachers can craft their remarks to include a statement of care about the student (which conveys, "You are seen"), along with an appreciation of their efforts (which conveys, "You have potential"). Students also experience feedback more positively when we add empathy, such as including "we" statements (which convey, "You are not alone"). Examples of "we" statements include "We can review two more examples to see how others did it" or "We can reread the section and see what we think."

QUICK START

	I can start this tomorrow!	I can begin this month	I need to discuss this with others	Resources needed
Identify stressful situations your class faces and do some situation crafting.				
Develop a group goal with your students to promote cohesion.				
Integrate empathetic feedback into conversations with students.				

CASE IN POINT:
MAKING THE PARKING LOT MORE WELCOMING

Right after Jeremiah Travers became the new principal at Palms Elementary School, he noticed that the drop-off and pick-up area was chaotic. It took a long time for people to get through the line, there was a lot of honking, and angry words were often exchanged. People were not following the rules and instead were entering the lot from both the exit lane as well as the entry lane. Sometimes people lingered, getting out of their cars to talk with someone else. Other times, students were dropped off across the street and darted between cars on their way through the parking lot into school.

Mr. Travers asked staff members about this, and they told him that one of the worst parts of their day was arrival. "Second only to dismissal, if you ask me," said one staff member. One teacher told Mr. Travers, "I stopped going to greet families/caregivers because it was so stressful for me to see what was happening." Another said, "I don't go to the drop-off area anymore because I don't want to contribute to the problem by having families/caregivers talk with me and not move along."

After some thought, Mr. Travers decided to contact the local police department for assistance. He explained that it was dangerous, and they were lucky someone had not been hurt. The police department sent two officers to staff the area. The officers had no specialized training in supporting schools but were used to crowd control. They were very strict about the rules and blew their whistle at people, pointed their radios at others, and wrote tickets to some. As a result, one of the parents commented, "We really don't feel welcome here. I'm looking for a new school because it's so bad. I'm treated like a criminal, and I'm just trying to get my kid to school on time."

What's Your Advice?

Mr. Travers could use some advice about situation crafting.

- What recommendations do you have for this team to create a welcoming—yet organized—drop-off and pick-up area?

- What role could teachers, parents, and other staff members play in this situation?

ESSENTIAL QUESTION

How does the environment and various situations convey a consistent message of welcoming?

THINK ABOUT

- Are students greeted each day?
- Do students, families/caregivers, and the community feel represented throughout the school?
- What transitioning situations do students experience that cause them anxiety about their belonging?

START – STOP – KEEP

Based on what you learned in this module, answer the questions that follow.

Start: What practice(s) would you like to start doing?

Stop: What practice(s) would you like to stop doing?

Keep: What practice(s) would you like to keep doing?

NOTES

"NOTHING ANNOYS PEOPLE
SO MUCH AS NOT
RECEIVING INVITATIONS."
- Oscar Wilde
The Importance of Being Earnest

2 INVITED

Being welcomed is an important aspect of the social contract between humans. But we can only be welcomed if we have been invited. Some students feel invited into their schools and classrooms; others do not. When students feel invited, they are more likely to experience belonging, which has a positive effect on learning and an effect size of 0.46.

Social exclusion, whether on a large or small scale, hurts. In fact, social exclusion is harmful to the health[1] and academic achievement[2] of our students in part because the learners do not have opportunities to collaborate with peers, complete homework together, or benefit from the systems of support that others can offer.

Schools can be intentional and ensure that all students feel invited. This includes classroom and extracurricular events. Who gets encouraged to try out for various sports teams? Who gets invited to social events? Who gets assigned to different classes and programs? Each of these are important considerations, and educators are wise to note how the invitations feel to those who receive them and those who do not.

Rachael is the parent of three school-aged children. She glowed when recounting her son Isaiah's receipt of a hand-addressed letter from the school. It was addressed to Isaiah, not his parents. Inside was a letter inviting him to apply to be a member of the safety patrol at his school. And, of course, he applied, and he takes his job very seriously: "Mom, we can't be late! I'm on crossing guard duty today!" But her true delight was in learning that *every* student in his grade received an invitation. Her son was not singled out because of some perceived leadership skill he was thought to possess. Instead, every student was given the opportunity to develop this set of skills. That's what being invited truly means.

HOW ARE WE PURSUING ALL STUDENTS' PRESENCE AND ACTIVELY EXTENDING NEW INVITATIONS?

Indicators: Teachers described the following indicators of a classroom and school environment where students feel the invitation to learn. Use these indicators to assess your own environment.

Table 2.1 • What Being Invited Looks, Sounds, and Feels Like

What Does It Look Like?	What Does It Sound Like?	What Does It Feel Like?
• Intentionally crafted environment and learning opportunities • Teacher modeling of inviting behavior • Sending emails and notes, making phone calls to families/caregivers to participate in learning and other school-related activities and events	• Using respectful language and tone in all interactions • Students and teachers using inviting language with others for academic and social opportunities on campus • Asking peers on the playground to join in play • Asking peers to sit with them during lunch or recess	• Wanted • Seen • Encouraged • Included • Consistent • Safe

TWO TRUTHS AND A LIE

Two of these statements are true; one is false. Can you spot the lie?

1. Social pain is detected and interpreted in a different region of the brain than physical pain.

2. Students who are disliked by the teacher are more readily rejected by peers than those who are liked by the teacher.

3. A predominant amount of instructional time during reading and math is spent doing independent seat work.

Did you spot the lie? Neural imaging studies reveal that social and physical pain are experienced in the same region of the brain. Social rejection can result in physical pain.[3] Ask any school nurse how frequently a student who is experiencing social exclusion or rejection comes to their office complaining about a stomachache or a headache. The somatic pain is real, but its cause may be social in nature.

The fact is that, at times, we as adults are the initial perpetrators of that pain. We disinvite students to learn through words and actions. Some are overt, such as the use of sarcasm with a targeted student. But more often, it is covert, as when we have fewer friendly actions with some students. We hold a pessimistic view of their learning potential and withdraw attention. This is not lost on their classmates, who can reliably report who the teacher likes and dislikes. Further, these classmates often adopt a similar dislike of the student.[4]

We further disinvite students from the learning process when we reduce the rigor of the content we teach. A study of the literacy assignments of 12 million students found that those in high-poverty schools had fewer experiences with grade-level work, even when they had already demonstrated mastery.[5] The number of assigned minutes of independent seatwork—estimated at 70 percent in one study—doesn't help in our efforts to invite students into learning.[6]

INVITATIONAL TEACHING

Our daily teaching practices—and the language we use when we teach—convey much about how inviting we are. The concept of invitational teaching is viewed through four prisms:[7]

- **Trust:** The ongoing relationships between the teacher and students
- **Respect:** The actions that communicate an understanding of everyone's autonomy, identity, and value to the learning community
- **Optimism:** The sense that the potential of each classroom member is untapped, and that every member of the classroom is responsible for finding ways to help others reach their potential
- **Intentionality:** The practices, policies, processes, and programs of classrooms and schools that are carefully designed to convey trust, respect, and optimism to all

The concept of invitational teaching has been transformative in making it possible for us to self-monitor our own practices. It scales across two dimensions:

- *Inviting* versus *uninviting*
- *Intentional* versus *unintentional*

Table 2.2 • Intentional and Unintentional Inviting and Uninviting

1. *Intentionally uninviting teachers . . .*	4. *Intentionally inviting teachers . . .*
• are judgmental and belittling	• are consistent and steady with students
• display little care or regard	• notice learning and struggle
• are uninterested in the lives and feelings of students	• respond regularly with feedback
• isolate themselves from school life	• seek to build, maintain, and repair relationships
• seek power over students	

Table 2.2 • Intentional and Unintentional Inviting and Uninviting (continued)

2. *Unintentionally uninviting teachers . . .*	3. *Unintentionally inviting teachers . . .*
• distance themselves from students	• are eager but unreflective
• have low expectations	• are energetic but rigid when facing problems
• don't feel effective, and blame students for shortcomings	• are unaware of what works in their practice, and why
• fail to notice student learning or struggle	• have fewer means for responding when student learning is resistant to their usual methods
• offer little feedback to learners	

Source: Adapted from Purkey and Novak (1996).

We believe there are relatively few *intentionally uninviting teachers* (Quadrant 1), but they are corrosive to their students and the school organization. They need and deserve supports and coaching to change their behaviors. We believe there are also *unintentionally inviting teachers* (Quadrant 3), who are enthusiastic but less reflective about their practice. That makes them more vulnerable to disappointment and adversity. They, too, deserve supports and coaching, before they become intentionally uninviting.

We all seek to be *intentionally inviting* teachers who are consistent, steady, and responsive (Quadrant 4). But there may be times when we find ourselves being *unintentionally uninviting* (Quadrant 2). We do so when we hold lower expectations for some students and distance ourselves from interactions. It is important that we not allow ourselves to be lulled into a false sense of complacency. Rather, we must see our invitations as specific to each student. The fact that we might be effectively inviting *some* students should not be confused as being invitational to *each* student.

TAKE ACTION

Develop and maintain trusting relationships with all your students. Trust runs both ways—we can't demand to know all our students while withholding ourselves. We aren't suggesting that you disclose everything about yourself. Rather, consider how they will get to know you as you get to know them.

(Continued)

(Continued)

Convey your respect for students in every action. Don't be the destructive teacher who says, "I'll give you the same kind of respect you give me." That sounds like a threat. We don't demand respect; we earn it. Instead, make sure that all your interactions are humane and growth-producing. Eye contact, tone of voice, and body language contribute to the message that you care, even when the going is a bit tougher for learners.

Show your optimism for students. Young people have the potential to change the world for the better; it's probably why you became a teacher in the first place. How will you demonstrate a "can do" spirit for them?

Use the 2x10 approach for hard-to-reach students.[8] For two minutes a day, for ten days in a row, talk to the student about anything *but* school. This process is used for students who need extra care and inviting into learning. Ask about something that is happening in their life and make a connection to your own experiences, if appropriate. More importantly, ask them a question about it. Reflect on changes you see after two weeks. Has your relationship improved?

QUICK START

	I can start this tomorrow!	I can begin this month	I need to discuss this with others	Resources needed
Select one area to strengthen to make you a more invitational teacher.				
Identify three ways you will share appropriate aspects of your life with your students.				
Identify a hard-to-reach student and try the 2x10 approach.				

HIGH EXPECTATIONS THROUGH GROUPING

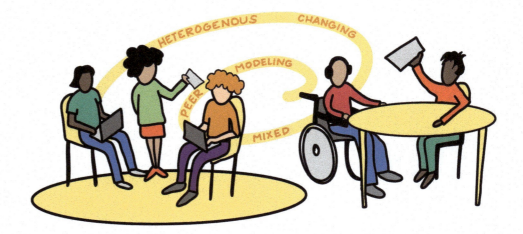

Collaborative learning is an essential part of a responsive instructional framework.[9] It can convey our intentionality about how we facilitate learning and what our expectations are for students. One major way we signal these expectations is through our grouping practices. The research on high-expectations teaching is significant, and one of the major findings is how grouping practices distinguish teachers with low expectations from their colleagues who hold an optimistic view of their students' potential.[10]

It turns out that teachers with lower expectations consistently use ability grouping and assign tasks to groups based on their achievement levels. In doing so, the pace of instruction slows down for low-achieving students, while higher-achieving students advance more quickly. The gap grows throughout the school year, further contributing to a lack of opportunity to learn.

On the other hand, teachers with high expectations use heterogenous groups of mixed abilities. As well, they change the grouping configurations monthly to promote peer relationships. They understand the importance of spreading effective learning approaches through peer modeling.

Another challenge of ability grouping is that those who are consistently in the lower-achieving group are given less responsibility for their learning. Instead, they get more directions that are repeated again and again. The tasks tend to be more skill-based and have less demand for application and transfer of learning using critical thinking. A lower quality of work is accepted by the teacher, who substitutes feedback with general encouragement. Overall, this allows students less room to make individual gains on learning goals.

TAKE ACTION

Use an alternate ranking system to ensure heterogeneity. Rank order students based on a major skill or disposition you are working toward. This may be academic, but it also may be one that involves student leadership. After listing the students from strongest to most in need of support, cut the list in half. If you have thirty-two students, you'll have one list for students 1–16 and another for students 17–32. Now take the first two from each list (students 1 and 2, plus students 17 and 18). That's a group. Repeat for the entire list. You'll have groups that have heterogeneity but are not stretched so far that the differences may be too much for the group to handle.

Figure 2.1 • Alternative Ranking System Sample

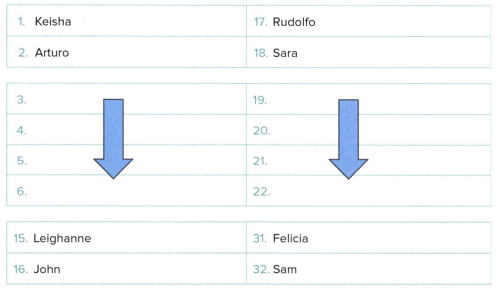

| 1. Keisha | 17. Rudolfo |
| 2. Arturo | 18. Sara |

3.	19.
4.	20.
5.	21.
6.	22.

| 15. Leighanne | 31. Felicia |
| 16. John | 32. Sam |

Source: Frey, Fisher, and Hattie (2018).

Plan for success. Start small by using/implementing heterogeneous groups, especially when students are new to each other. Keep the group tasks to between five to fifteen minutes, adjusting for developmental and academic readiness levels. Take notes about what's working and what needs improvement. Make sure there are clear learning intentions and success criteria for the group so that they will be more likely to be successful.

Keep track of who has had opportunities to work with others. Keep a spreadsheet so you can see which peers each student has had an opportunity to work with. It can be easy to settle into a comfortable pattern for too long, so schedule group changes at the end of units of instruction. If you're finding that groups are looking too similar, ask yourself whether you are over-relying on one metric (like reading scores) and under-relying on others (prosocial skills, such as sharing).

QUICK START

	I can start this tomorrow!	I can begin this month	I need to discuss this with others	Resources needed
Identify when you will use heterogeneous groups throughout the day or the period.				
Determine a metric you will use to develop an alternative ranking system.				
Schedule reminders in your calendar to switch groups.				

THE OPPORTUNITY TO LEARN

You can't learn what you haven't been taught.

Did you know that the systematic exposure to less challenging curricula leads to depressed academic achievement over time? There's even a name for this phenomenon: the opportunity to learn. It begins in elementary school, where some students spend more time on the development of discrete reading and mathematics skills but receive fewer chances to apply these across the curriculum, including in science, social studies, the arts, and physical education. They may even be retained in a grade, a widespread practice in elementary school that has failed to show evidence of impact. In fact, ten meta-analyses of a total of 339 studies have failed to reveal a single positive effect size, which is a statistical measure of impact on learning.[11] The effect size of grade-level retention is actually −0.29. Talk about disinviting: *You're not invited to first grade, kid. Sorry.*

It continues in middle school, where well-intentioned administrators assign students who are not making expected progress to double-periods of intervention. Other courses, often in the visual and performing arts, are removed from their schedules. What this approach sacrifices is knowledge building, a known predictor of higher reading comprehension for adolescents.[12] In the meantime, they fall further behind their peers in knowledge gained in other subjects. For these students, the gap continues to grow in high school. The disparities in college preparatory course enrollment for students of color, students living in poverty, students with disabilities, foster youth, and multilingual learners are significant.[13]

In order to address this, some innovative middle and high schools have taken steps to rectify it, including the following actions:

1. Developing strong transition plans between levels of school so that students feel belonging to their new school (such as elementary students visiting their middle schools)[14]

2. Staging recruitment campaigns to invite students to take more rigorous coursework

3. Removing access barriers, such as a required teacher recommendation to enroll in advanced coursework

4. Providing additional supports for students who may struggle in those courses

By strengthening the pipeline across a student's K–12 academic career, we can invite them into a more rigorous learning space.

TAKE ACTION

Use targeted small-group instruction to pre-teach. Monitor progress of students regularly, and respond when you find some students struggling. Plan short pre-teaching sessions for students who aren't making expected progress to "warm up" a text for them in advance of whole-group instruction. This approach gives learners the further advantage of benefiting from your Tier 1 instruction.

Schedule regular intervals for reteaching. Plan fifteen-minute Mastery Monday sessions for students to regroup about a topic of their choice from the previous week. Have students reconfigure in small groups to reexamine a problem or task they had difficulty with, and encourage them to work together to strengthen their knowledge. Provide scaffolds and direct instruction as needed so that the group is successful. Students who didn't have a struggle can serve as peer tutors.

QUICK START

	I can start this tomorrow!	I can begin this month	I need to discuss this with others	Resources needed
Use encouraging language with all students about their ability to strive.				
Invite elementary students to tour the feeder middle and high school they will attend in the future so they can see the many opportunities that await them.				
Add discussion of the importance of advanced course enrollment to every middle and high school conference with families/caregivers, including IEP meetings.				

CASE IN POINT: INVITING ALL STUDENTS

During a team meeting, third-grade teacher Araceli Ramirez said, "I see a group of students get on a school bus about two blocks from here, but they don't come to our school. Does anyone know where they're going?"

Her colleague, Justin Kempt, responded, "Yeah, they go to a regional program for students with disabilities. Their parents were given choices by the school system, and they decided to go someplace else."

Ms. Ramirez was shocked. "Why would they not want to be here? It's a great school with lots of supports. Maybe nobody from the school ever invited them into our school, and their parents didn't know how amazing we are. They really should be invited to our school."

Mr. Kempt agreed. He suggested they speak with Mr. Green, the new principal. "Maybe he would be interested. We do have space at our school, and it would be great to have our students get to know kids with more significant disabilities."

A few weeks later, Mr. Green sent a letter home to the thirty-two students who would have been enrolled in the school but were instead attending other schools. Some of these students were those identified with disabilities who were attending the regional program, and others had families/caregivers who had exercised other choice options. In his letter, Mr. Green outlined the benefits of the school, and he invited students and their families/caregivers to come for a visit and meet the staff.

The result? Twenty-eight of the thirty-two families/caregivers were so impressed with the invitation that they accepted and enrolled their children in the local school. As one parent said, "We feel so invited and cared for. I know my son is going to be better off connecting with other kids who live in our neighborhood."

What's Your Advice?

- What recommendations do you have for supporting the students who will be enrolling based on the invitation?

- What systems should be in place to ensure that students feel invited every year?

- Are there students who should be attending your school who should be invited?

ESSENTIAL QUESTION

How are we pursuing all students' presence and actively extending new invitations?

THINK ABOUT

- In what ways is invitational teaching part of your daily instruction?
- How do students experience opportunities to learn in your classroom?
- How have your grouping practices evolved to convey high expectations for all?

START – STOP – KEEP

Based on what you learned in this module, answer the questions that follow.

Start: What practice(s) would you like to start doing?

Stop: What practice(s) would you like to stop doing?

Keep: What practice(s) would you like to keep doing?

NOTES

3 PRESENT

It's hard to belong if you are not present. Presence is both physical and emotional. In this module, we'll focus on the physical presence of students. In later modules, we'll address emotional presence. There are many reasons why students are not present in school—including attendance, bullying, and disciplinary actions, to name a few.

There are also access issues, such as enrollment in specific classes. There are some schools that segregate students with disabilities or multilingual learners or students identified as gifted and talented. Sometimes students must earn the right to enter the classroom based on unfair or unclear behavioral criteria, such as being suspended for an infraction. We have never understood the logic that being barred from a class for a few days somehow fixes whatever was wrong in the first place.

There are also places in the school building where students are not allowed, labeled with signs such as "Keep out!" or "No students beyond this point!" Some middle schools, in an effort to curb bullying or exposure to discussion of more mature content, even designate specific locations for sixth graders to sit during lunch apart from the seventh and eighth graders. While seemingly well intentioned, these scenarios send powerful messages about where students can be present.

Essential Question:

HOW DO WE ENSURE THAT ALL STUDENTS ARE PRESENT FOR LEARNING?

Indicators: Teachers described these indicators of a classroom and school environment that are intentional about creating a place where students are present. Use these indicators to assess your own environment.

Table 3.1 · What Being Present Looks, Sounds, and Feels Like

What Does It Look Like?	What Does It Sound Like?	What Does It Feel Like?
• Having students' physical bodies on campus and in class • Being involved in clubs or campus groups • Being mentally present • Demonstrating active listening skills • Giving students opportunities to be involved • Providing opportunities to make up missed assignments	• Students participating in productive, student-driven conversations • Using welcoming language when students return to school • Using enthusiastic greetings ("I'm happy you're here today!") • Engaging in detailed conversations	• Valued • Soothed • Calm • Appreciated • Held in high regard

TWO TRUTHS AND A LIE

Two of these statements are true; one is false. Can you spot the lie?

1. Suspension and expulsion rates show overrepresentation of some student groups.
2. Chronic absenteeism is more concerning in the upper grade levels.
3. Fifteen percent of all enrolled students in the United States have an identified disability.

Students need to be present in school for the learning experiences created for them to take hold. Yet several barriers can get in the way. Chronic absenteeism, defined as missing 10 percent of the school year (excused or unexcused), is on the rise, especially post-pandemic. Many school districts, regardless of income level or demographics of the student population, are struggling to get their attendance rates back to pre-pandemic levels. Primary students are especially impacted. Chronically absent youngsters have lower reading achievement in third grade than their peers who are present in school.[1]

But discipline systems that exclude students exacerbate this. Black students, males, LGBTQIA+ students, and students with disabilities are overrepresented in the data.[2] This is not linked to the level of school poverty or type of school attended. These practices added an additional 11 million days of lost instruction in the 2015–2016 school year, further exacerbating an already dire crisis of chronic absenteeism.[3]

Even if students are regularly attending, it is difficult for them to experience true belonging when they are educated in segregated settings within the school or district. Nearly one out of six students has a disability, yet too often they do not experience learning with nondisabled peers.[4] Students with disabilities who are educated in general education classrooms demonstrate greater gains in language development, higher levels of engagement, and more satisfying and diverse friendships; they are also more socially competent.[5]

The lie? "Chronic absenteeism is more concerning in the upper grade levels." In reality, chronic absenteeism is of great concern at *every* grade level.

ATTENDANCE

Getting students to school is a shared responsibility between families/caregivers and educators. We all tend to forget the impact that missing a few days has on access to instruction. Students who miss more than eighteen days of school in kindergarten and first grade are less likely to read on grade level by third grade.[6] For older students, being chronically absent is strongly associated with failing at school and dropping out of school.[7]

Table 3.2 • Attendance Rates and Instruction Days Missed

95% attendance	9 days missed – nearly two weeks
90% attendance	18 days missed – more than three weeks
85% attendance	27 days missed – more than five weeks
80% attendance	36 days missed – more than seven weeks

Missing school has a negative effect size of −0.37, meaning that it's harmful to learning and can result in students losing ground academically.

Figure 3.1 · Effect Size for Missing School

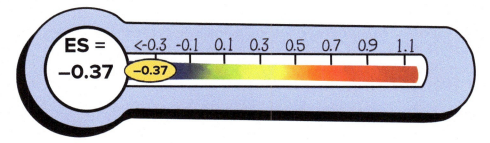

In addition, being absent impacts students' sense of belonging because while other students are in school interacting with each other, absent students are missing out on those opportunities by not being present in school. For example, students with chronic health conditions who miss school due to their medical needs report lower scores of perceived belonging, and they may end up not feeling very good about themselves.[8] These results seem to generalize, as students who are not attending school for whatever reason report a reduced sense of belonging, which likely contributes to their poor achievement.

TAKE ACTION

Welcome students back. When a student returns from being absent, let them know that they were missed. About half of students surveyed believe that they are not missed by their teachers when they are absent.[9] The same practice can be used for students who come late to school. Make sure they know that you are happy to see them and that their presence makes the class more complete.

Provide make-up support. Hold students accountable for the learning they missed, yet provide support for them to be successful. If learners don't think that they'll miss anything, attendance will suffer. If they think they're too far behind to catch up, they'll miss more. One way to do this is to keep a record of each day's work/notes (digitally or hard copy) so that students know what they need to complete when they return.

(Continued)

(Continued)

Model excellent attendance. There is a correlation between teacher attendance and student attendance. Be at school as often as possible, and let students know when you are working in another location, such as attending a professional learning event.

Monitor attendance. Review data regularly and identify which students are out. Talk with your colleagues about actions that team members can take to address attendance, such as home visits, personal contact with family members or caregivers, or wake-up calls. Display the data—such as percentages by grade or class—in prominent areas to raise awareness.

Set short-term interim attendance goals. Create reasonable attendance goals with individual students who are chronically absent or tardy and their families/caregivers to steadily improve. Celebrate when the goals are met so that students recognize that their efforts are making a difference.

Minimize obstacles. Talk with students and their families/caregivers to figure out why students are missing school. Then, work to remove those barriers, such as bullying, clean clothes, reliable transportation, or sibling care.

QUICK START

	I can start this tomorrow!	I can begin this month	I need to discuss this with others	Resources needed
Analyze attendance data for your class, including excused absences and tardies, to identify students who are chronically absent.				
Create a reminder note so you can welcome back students who were absent the day before.				
Make a plan to contact families/caregivers of students in your class who are chronically absent to find out how the school can help.				

SUSPENSION AND EXPULSION

Telling students that they cannot attend school because of their actions and behaviors worsens attendance and threatens students' sense of belonging. It also negatively impacts their learning, at least as measured by grade point averages.[10] They come to believe that their membership, or presence, has contingencies and can be revoked at any time. Remember that most behavior is an adaptation to the situation, and we can craft situations and responses that do not provoke certain behaviors or that deescalate behavior.

Here are some key takeaways from studies of suspension and expulsion:[11,12]

- Students have lost millions of days of instructional time due to out-of-school suspensions.
- Educators continue to suspend students with disabilities at much higher rates than their nondisabled peers.
- Racial disparities in suspension have persisted across the years.
- Suspending students does little to reduce future misbehavior.
- Suspensions do *not* result in improved academic achievement for peers or perceptions of positive school climate.

Of course, severe infractions should be addressed within the legal framework and appropriate consequences applied. In these cases, suspension is likely part of the reaction from the school system, but students must understand the impact of their actions if they are to change their behavior. Importantly, the work done after a suspension is what helps students learn, and that work can help repair the feeling of isolation, shame, or fractured belonging that comes from being sent away from school.

Suspension data suggests that students are more often suspended for minor offenses, ambiguous infractions, and general disruptions.[13,14] In these cases, there are a host of alternatives that should be implemented so that learning days are not lost, and students understand that their presence is valued even as their behavior needs to change.

TAKE ACTION

Use impromptu conversations. Questions such as the following can be used to help the student understand the impact of their actions:[15]

- **Tell the story:** "What happened? I'd like to hear your story first."
- **Explore the harm:** "Who do you think has been affected?"
- **Repair the harm:** "What needs to happen so that it can be right again?"
- **Reach an agreement:** "What help do you need to do so?"
- **Plan a follow-up:** "What's a good time to check in with you to see how you're doing?"

Note that sometimes we need to take a pause or a deep breath before we ask these questions so we can intentionally adjust to a caring tone.

Use contracts and agreements. Meeting with an individual student and developing an agreement can help them make decisions about how to respond when a situation is challenging. Generally, contracts include the goals for targeted behavior, alternatives or expectations, rewards, and recording method.

(Continued)

(Continued)

Figure 3.2 · Contract Sample

My Contract:
Name: _____
Date: _____
These are my goals:
1.
_____
_____
2.
_____
_____
3.
_____
_____
These are my consequences if I don't meet my goals:
_____
_____
_____
_____
There are my rewards/reinforcers if I meet my goals:
_____
_____
My contract will be reviewed on:
_____
_____
Signatures: _____
_____
_____

 Available for download at **resources.corwin.com/belongingplaybook**

Provide mini-courses or counseling. Sometimes students need more support for their behavioral growth, just like some students need more support for academic development. Students may need to be referred to counseling, or they may need to participate in a mini-course to learn some replacement behaviors. These mini-courses can be implemented by teachers or support staff, and they often include readings and reflection journals appropriate for the students' age.

Create reentry plans. Anytime a student is removed from a class based on problematic behavior, there should be clear plans for that student's return to the learning environment. Simply showing up in class again does not address students' need to belong. Students need to rehearse how they will return, who they can go to if the situation is stressful, what actions/behaviors they will display on return, and when they will check in with a specific adult. Make sure all of the adults involved in the situation are aware of the plan and the goal to return the student to learning while strengthening that student's sense of belonging.

QUICK START

	I can start this tomorrow!	I can begin this month	I need to discuss this with others	Resources needed
Analyze suspension or expulsion data for your class to seek patterns or trends.				
Identify common problematic behaviors that result in students being sent to the office.				
Notice how, when, and with whom you use impromptu conversations to deescalate problematic behaviors in your classroom.				

INCLUSIVE PRACTICES

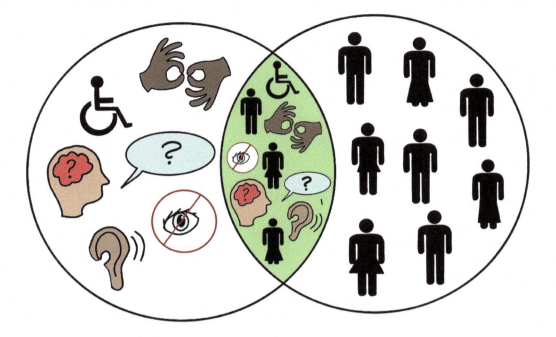

Full membership in a community requires being present in the daily flow of activities. This is both an ethical and a legal dimension of the Individuals with Disabilities Education Improvement Act, commonly called IDEIA.[16] The requirement is that students with disabilities (SWD), to the greatest extent possible, are educated alongside peers without disabilities.

This principle has been validated time and again in court cases, but the spirit of the law isn't always manifested. Too often, the starting point for school teams is a segregated setting. Only then are any possibilities about general education even considered. The result of this flawed decision-making model is predictable: limited general education access, especially for students with intellectual disabilities.[17]

Until 1974, SWDs were often denied any kind of schooling whatsoever: *exclusion*. Even today, many SWDs experience *segregation* in separate classrooms or separate schools. There are many SWDs who experience *integration*; they are clustered in a general education classroom but largely educated as a separate group. Students who experience true *inclusion* are full members of the classroom, socially and academically.

This diagram can be further interpreted through the lens of race, ethnicity, language, or gender. What unintended messages are telegraphed to children and the community at large when we preserve systems that formally determine who belongs and who doesn't?

TAKE ACTION

Learn more about inclusive practices. If you are a general educator, ask to meet with special educators at your school to learn more about inclusive practices. If you are a special educator, ask to meet with your general education colleagues to do the same. The purpose of the meeting should be on strengthening inclusive practices.

Update language. Language is power, and it signals how we value others. Do we commonly discuss students as possessions: *your* students versus *my* students? Be conscious of using *our students* instead to signal collective responsibility. Use gender inclusive language, whenever possible. For example, try "good morning, scholars" instead of "good morning, boys and girls." Be mindful of using people-first language by acknowledging the overriding value of personhood, not allowing the nature of the disability to define the person. A *student has autism spectrum disorder*; they are not *autistic*. Note that the student is first and the disability is identified later, if needed.

Implement accommodations and modifications per the IEP. Every IEP includes agreed adaptations to the curriculum and is tailored to the individual to ensure that the learner can benefit from their educational experiences. Review students' accommodations and/or modifications periodically to ensure you are living up to this legal contract.

Support paraprofessionals. Special education paraprofessionals are an important part of the system of supports for some SWDs. If you are a general educator, welcome them into your classroom, and afford them the membership status they deserve as colleagues. Advocate for their continued professional learning, especially in their participation in schoolwide professional learning events. And don't refer to them as "my paraprofessional." They're not possessions, either!

QUICK START

	I can start this tomorrow!	I can begin this month	I need to discuss this with others	Resources needed
Assess how SWDs in your classroom are doing in terms of belonging.				
Meet with your special or general education colleagues to learn more about inclusive practices.				
Learn about the school or district committees that have been formed to support special education in your community. Identify what role you can play in being more actively involved.				

CASE IN POINT: ATTENDANCE HUDDLES

Seaside Middle School's attendance team "huddles up" every morning within the first hour of school. These are standing fifteen-minute meetings that happen every day, and all team members who are physically able to do so stand for the duration. ("The meetings are faster that way," says the assistant principal.) The team includes an administrator, a school counselor, the special education coordinator, and a classroom teacher. All of them have been trained in restorative practices, which are implemented schoolwide. The classroom teacher is a rotation position, whereas the others attend daily. The teacher rotates daily by grade level, and who goes to the meeting is determined by their grade-level team.

The attendance huddle agenda remains the same each day:

- Review an update on yesterday's actions agreed on at the huddle.

- Share students of concern for today.

- Share knowledge about the students and pose questions.

- Determine an action and assign a team member to oversee the action.

The attendance clerk leads these meetings. Because the attendance clerk has a broad view of patterns and complexities, it is a natural choice. As the clerk says, "I'm the first point of contact for many students and their families."

One morning, which was pretty typical, the team discussed the previous day's actions: a home visit for one student, the scheduling of two family/caregiver conferences, and an individual meeting with a chronically tardy student. Then the attendance clerk spotlighted three students of concern:

- A seventh-grade student who had transferred to Seaside Middle School two weeks earlier but had already missed three days of school. A parent had called the student in sick each time.

- A sixth-grade student with a disability who had missed a portion of their first-period class twelve times during the first month of school due to tardiness.

- An eighth-grade student who had been involved in a verbal altercation several days earlier with another student. The eighth grader had not returned to school, and phone calls to the family/caregivers had gone unanswered.

What's Your Advice?

- What questions or follow-up actions would you advise for this team?

  o For the new transfer student?

  o For the chronically tardy student?

  o For the student who disappeared after an incident?

ESSENTIAL QUESTION

How do we ensure that all students are present for learning?

THINK ABOUT

- How do you communicate the expectation that students are present in the learning environment?

- How do you respond when students are absent or tardy?

- What procedures can you implement to address problematic behavior so that students' sense of belonging is not compromised as they learn new social and behavioral skills?

- How do you advocate for students with disabilities to be supported in regular classes?

START – STOP – KEEP

Based on what you learned in this module, answer the questions that follow.

Start: What practice(s) would you like to start doing?
Stop: What practice(s) would you like to stop doing?
Keep: What practice(s) would you like to keep doing?

NOTES

4 ACCEPTED

After the signing of the Good Friday Agreement in 1998, Northern Ireland faced the dilemma of how to build acceptance between sectarian factions that had been involved in deadly conflict for decades. Schools typically reflect the attitudes of the larger society, and no schools in the country had ever educated Catholic and Protestant youth together. In fact, still to this day, most schools in that area are segregated by religion. However, an increasing number of them are transforming themselves into integrated schools, driven by parents who want their children to experience a more diversified education. Interviews with elementary and secondary students in these transformed schools revealed the following actions their teachers took to build acceptance among children:[1]

- Open and frank discussion of differences through awareness and acceptance
- School signage and emblems signaling acceptance of all
- Changes in extracurricular activities to promote contact with others
- Changes in instruction to promote sharing skills and peer learning
- Curricular changes to increase opportunities to learn about self and others

Importantly, these transformed schools seek to help students learn about themselves as well as others; they know that naively homogenizing students would mute the unique identities that are their individual strengths.

Being accepted is a crucial feature of school connectedness, which is the belief students have that teachers and classmates care about them as individuals and about their learning.[2] Higher reported school connectedness among families/caregivers and students is associated with better attendance and participation in school functions. It is also associated with student wellness, and it's an indicator of the health of the school climate.[3]

HOW ARE WE RECEIVING ALL LEARNERS UNCONDITIONALLY AND GRACIOUSLY?

Indicators: Teachers described these indicators of a classroom and school environment where students feel accepted. Use these indicators to assess your own environment.

Table 4.1 • What Being Accepted Looks, Sounds, and Feels Like

What Does It Look Like?	What Does It Sound Like?	What Does It Feel Like?
• Including all students • Allowing students to build autonomy to make choices and decisions • Using open body language • Using appropriate physical contact (e.g., hugs, handshakes, eye contact, smiles) • Celebrating differences, and incorporating them into the classroom community and learning activities	• Allowing for open sharing of ideas • Encouraging genuine questions (personal and academic) • Expressing authentic concern and interest • Challenging stigmas or biases	• Comfortable • Open • Seen • Knowing you're missed • Understood • Transparent • Included • Valued

TWO TRUTHS AND A LIE

Two of these statements are true; one is false. Can you spot the lie?

1. Long-term interactions are one of the best ways to promote attitude changes in students about their acceptance of peers who are different from them.
2. Students who experience a high degree of acceptance are more able to adjust to learning situations, such as entry into a new school setting.
3. By the time students get to high school, teacher and parent acceptance has less impact on academic achievement.

If you spotted the lie as being the third statement, you're getting really good at this! Adolescents thrive on the unconditional acceptance of their families/caregivers and teachers. When acceptance is conditional (what learners *do* versus who they *are*), students begin to doubt whether they are truly accepted by the important adults in their lives. Adolescents who experience conditional acceptance by teachers perceive the learning environment as less secure, and they have a lower sense of autonomy.[4]

School connectedness is a protective factor for young people, which means they are less likely to engage in unhealthy behaviors. One study found that an adolescent's sense of school connectedness predicted the following:[5]

- Substance use
- School absenteeism
- Early sexual initiation
- Violence
- Risk of unintentional injury (e.g., drinking and driving, not wearing seatbelts)

Acceptance by and of others is linked to school satisfaction. In fact, students often name their peer relationships as the primary valued aspect of schooling.[6] But acceptance of others doesn't just happen. There is strong evidence that regular contact among groups of people has a positive long-term effect on acceptance across identities, including racial, ethnic, religious, ability, LGBTQIA+, and language differences.[7] Teachers promote such experiences by ensuring that students regularly interact with one another in a variety of academic and school-based social situations, such as recess and lunch.[8] In addition, they further promote interactions by utilizing curriculum materials that promote learning about others.

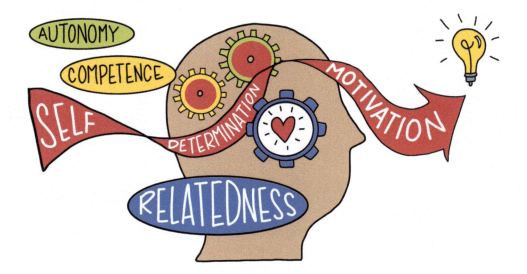

SELF-DETERMINATION AND RELATEDNESS

To be able to accept others, students must first be able to accept themselves. An important dimension of self-acceptance involves self-determination, the ability to make sensible decisions about their own lives. This is not the same as self-sufficiency, since children need many years, often into adulthood, to live independently. However, they grow each year in their ability to do so, acquiring the skills they need to reach their aspirations. Schools play a pivotal role in developing the self-determination of young people.

Self-determination is a mindset. Self-determination theory relies on three dimensions:[9]

- *Autonomy* to make choices and decisions, which contributes to a sense of agency to achieve goals

- *Competence* to demonstrate skills and develop new ones

- *Relatedness* to others through social bonding, which prevents feeling alone

When these conditions are present, motivation increases. And motivation has an effect size of 0.42. But the interesting thing is that relatedness comes *before* motivation; it fuels the learning engine. Relatedness, which is feeling connected to others, including teachers and peers, is a prerequisite. When relatedness is absent, self-determination is threatened. With the decline of self-determination comes reduced motivation to learn. Feeling accepted, therefore, is key to relatedness.

TAKE ACTION

Teach students about what is in their control and what is out of their control. Self-determination doesn't mean always having things go our way. Young people can struggle with what they can and cannot control, and this can be a source of frustration for them. Use a simple visual to teach about where they can best influence their own lives.

Figure 4.1 • Self-Determination Visual

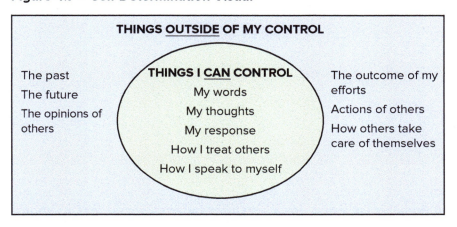

THINGS <u>OUTSIDE</u> OF MY CONTROL

The past
The future
The opinions of others

THINGS I <u>CAN</u> CONTROL

My words
My thoughts
My response
How I treat others
How I speak to myself

The outcome of my efforts
Actions of others
How others take care of themselves

(Continued)

(Continued)

Write letters home to students about their efforts and accomplishments.
Adopt a schoolwide practice of writing notes of appreciation home to
students to highlight their persistence toward goals. These "grit letters" are
handwritten and addressed to the student, not to the family/caregivers. These
letters give families/caregivers positive topics to discuss, and they increase
relatedness and school connectedness.

Use a Banking Time approach with hard-to-reach students. This approach,
which works best for young students, calls for short (five- to ten-minute) one-
to-one play sessions with a child.[10] Some students self-silence because they
have learned from past experiences not to express personal stories, making
it more difficult to build connections. This intervention has been shown to
increase relatedness to the teacher among young children while decreasing
problematic behaviors. Banking Time sessions are play-oriented and directed
by the student. Rather than teaching and giving directions, the teacher
facilitates conversation and narrates what is occurring, providing the child
with ways of being able to build language by labeling feelings. There
are four components to the session: 1) observing the child's actions;
2) narrating the child's actions; 3) labeling the child's feelings and emotions;
and 4) developing relational themes.

QUICK START

	I can start this tomorrow!	I can begin this month	I need to discuss this with others	Resources needed
Provide time in class daily or weekly for you and your students to share personal experiences and news.				
Build choice into tasks so that students can exercise their autonomy.				
Invite students to make personal connections to the topics of study.				

CULTURALLY SUSTAINING PEDAGOGIES

Being accepted into the learning culture of school requires that the learning is grounded in the lives of students. Culturally sustaining pedagogies (CSP) are an approach to teaching and learning designed to move youth forward in their learning by shifting from a deficit-based education to an assets-based education. Culturally sustaining pedagogies are the product of the instructional and curricular choices a school makes, and they serve as the heart of the work on belonging. Culturally sustaining pedagogies "ask educators to see young people as 'whole versus broken' when they enter our classrooms."[11] This approach requires that we see students as assets, recognize their strengths, and develop an academic line of inquiry that is additive, rather than subtractive.[12] In doing so, we send a clear message that they are accepted as members of the learning community.

Culturally sustaining pedagogies seek to address this question: *How do our students learn about themselves and the world?* To do so requires that schooling help students answer questions as they continuously construct and understand their identities. In addition, it requires that school organizations become culturally sustaining. Here are a few examples:

- Young children from the Stoney Nakoda community in Canada studied Indigenous storytelling as a gateway to early literacy development.[13]

- Third- and fourth-grade multilingual students created bilingual picture books to use with younger students, while boosting their own reading and writing skills.[14]

- Black mentors from a local university were paired with Black middle school boys in an afterschool STEM program designed with them in mind.[15]

- A high school intervention team revamped their problem-solving approach by using a culturally responsive decision-making model that considered access to culturally sustaining pedagogy quality core curriculum, conducted student and family/caregiver interviews, and added these findings to the conventional academic data they utilized.[16]

TAKE ACTION

***T*ake an inventory of curriculum materials.** Locate existing materials that profile people and authors from across the spectrum of human experience. In addition to race, ethnicity, and language, look for representation of people with disabilities, LGBTQIA+ people, and multiracial people. Then look at whether their presence serves to elevate. As an example, too often characters with disabilities play a secondary and passive role and are there only to make the other characters better people. Identify gaps you have unearthed, and supplement to ensure students are represented. The American Library Association provides a book list: https://www.ala.org/advocacy/literacy/inclusive-booklists.

Teach about contrastive grammars in language. Students who speak languages other than English, as well as those who use dialects of English, often wrongly believe that their language is of lesser value. Teach students about the rule-bound grammars of their languages and dialects, and how they are useful in different situations. This allows for the positioning of standard and nonstandard grammars as useful and appropriate in different settings, including school, home, and community.

(Continued)

(Continued)

Table 4.2 • New Ways of Talking About Language: From "Error" to "Pattern"[17]

Instead of This	Try This
Thinking in terms of • Proper or improper • Good or bad	Seeing language as • Appropriate or inappropriate • Effective or ineffective in a specific setting
Talking about • Right or wrong • Correct or incorrect	Talking about • Patterns • How language varies by setting
Thinking that students • Make mistakes or errors • Have problems with plurals, possessives, tenses, etc. • Leave off -s, -es, -ed	See your students as • Following the grammar patterns of their home language
Saying students • "Should have" or "Are supposed to," "Need to," "Should correct"	Inviting students to • Codeswitch (choose the language pattern to fit the setting)
Making red notes in the margin • Correcting students' grammar	Leading students to • Compare and contrast languages • Build on existing knowledge to add new knowledge—standard English • Codeswitch to fit the setting

QUICK START

	I can start this tomorrow!	I can begin this month	I need to discuss this with others	Resources needed
Add cultural artifacts to your classroom that reflect your students' lives.				
Share your major topics for the year, and survey families/caregivers to gauge their interest and willingness in being a guest speaker.				
Reexamine curriculum for opportunities to teach grammar contrastively.				

CHALLENGING STIGMAS

Stigmas are judgments used to indicate that an individual or a group does not conform to cultural norms. Not all differences carry a stigma. However, "when elements of labeling, stereotyping, separation, status loss and discrimination occur together in a power situation that allows them," acceptance is threatened.[18] When teachers do not label students, with evidence drawn from the disability community, the effect size is 0.61, suggesting that the labels become a stigma that follows the students and contributes to lower expectations for students' learning.

Stigmas that are accompanied by silence are especially damaging. If no one talks about it, isolation grows. Stigmas in schools mirror those held by the larger society. Race, ethnicity, language, ability, gender identity, gender expression, sexual orientation, religion, size, and mental health status are the most common stigmas found in the K–12 population. These negative judgments by others can turn into internal stigmatizing. Students who are targets of these negative judgments are less likely to seek aid, further jeopardizing their physical and mental health.

Caring educators do much to address stigmas, although not all these attempts are useful or productive. As an example, disability simulations that require students to temporarily adapt to a sensory or physical disability to promote understanding have been shown to have little positive effect.[19] Indeed, some disability rights advocates assert that these promote an ableist culture where disability is only understood as a subtractive.[20]

One source of stigma that occurs across every group is mental health status, as educators are well aware. Persistent sadness and hopelessness among school-aged youth was up 40 percent in 2021 compared to the previous decade.[21] And depression has a negative impact on learning, with an effect size of −0.29. A study of 290,000 people over nine years, controlling for genetic risks, suggests that quality sleep is the greatest protective factor against depression and that frequent social connection reduced the risk of depression by 18 percent.[22] Now more than ever, students must understand that they are not invisible, and they need their teachers to notice and address their needs. Educators are the eyes and ears of the mental health system and are often the first to notice when a student needs help.

TAKE ACTION

Identify and address personal biases. Examine your own thinking, and the judgments you make based on your upbringing, so that you can reduce stigmatizing others. Observe your language and identify terminology that you use that may be based on stereotypes. Consider taking implicit association tests (e.g., implicit.harvard.edu/implicit/takeatest.html) to identify potential biases.

Model respect for people who are affected by mental health difficulties. Don't use words like *lame*, *crazy*, *nuts*, and *insane* to disparage others or to describe something you dislike. Your words impact colleagues and students.

Teach mental health literacy. Examine your curriculum to identify places where lessons about mental health are aligned to the topic of study. These might include physical and mental wellness, transitioning to middle or high school, developing skills to address stress and anxiety, or supporting friends who are struggling.

Build the mental health awareness of families/caregivers. Advocate for events that provide information about mental health. Workshops that partner school personnel with respected community leaders are especially useful. These do not need to be stand-alone events! Integrate distribution of informational materials at Back to School Nights, Literacy and Math Nights, and sporting events.

Be aware of the signs of suicide. Suicide rates have increased, even in children as young as five to eleven years of age.[23] Suicide is the second leading cause of death for people ages ten to fourteen.[24] The signs that indicate a young person is considering suicide include the following:[25]

- Changes in eating and sleeping behaviors
- Alcohol and drug use
- Withdrawal from friends and family/caregivers
- Neglect of personal appearance
- Lack of response to praise
- Irritability
- Sadness or crying spells
- Posts on social media suggesting feelings of isolation or depression
- Talking about or otherwise indicating plans to commit suicide or self-harm

QUICK START

	I can start this tomorrow!	I can begin this month	I need to discuss this with others	Resources needed
Normalize seeking help by making sure school-based wellness services are featured in your classroom.				
Counter myths that are expressed with facts to help your students understand stigmas.				
Learn the indicators that students need mental health assistance and identify where to refer them for that help.				

CASE IN POINT: DADS AND DONUTS

Oakdale Elementary School holds a book fair in the campus library every spring. It is one of the main fundraisers for the school, and it gives the opportunity for teachers and students to purchase new books. In the past, the school has designated one morning during the book fair as "Dads and Donuts," where students can bring their fathers before school to shop at the book fair and receive a free donut. This was always a well-attended morning, and the school was proud that so many fathers would come to campus when that wasn't the norm for a typical morning drop-off.

This year, however, the teachers and staff at Oakdale decided to redesignate the name of the event. They had examined their schoolwide practices at the close of the previous year in order to assess them for inclusion and acceptance. They discussed how Dads and Donuts excluded a variety of families/caregivers across their student population, and they didn't want that exclusion to continue. Moving forward, they chose to call the event "Donuts with Grownups," so that students had the opportunity to bring any adult with them to the book fair on that special morning and receive a donut.

What's Your Advice?

- Although "Dads and Donuts" brought many fathers to school who didn't otherwise come to campus in the morning, in what ways could that event make others feel rejected or unwelcome at the school? How might the students who didn't have a father or father figure in their life feel when the school promoted this event?

- In what ways will the new "Donuts with Grownups" event foster acceptance for families/caregivers across the school?

WHAT'S NEXT?

ESSENTIAL QUESTION

How are we receiving all learners unconditionally and graciously?

THINK ABOUT

- In what ways are you building self-determination and relatedness in the classroom?
- How are you seeking input from students and families/caregivers to strengthen culturally sustaining curriculum?
- Are your efforts to address stigmas delivering intended outcomes?

START – STOP – KEEP

Based on what you learned in this module, answer the questions that follow.

Start: What practice(s) would you like to start doing?

Stop: What practice(s) would you like to stop doing?

Keep: What practice(s) would you like to keep doing?

KNOWN

What does it mean to feel known? Being known refers to "the belief that others have developed accurate opinions of one's traits and characteristics."[1] Psychologists have described the desire to be known by others as a deeply rooted need among humans. In the classroom, the other dimensions of belonging become easier to implement the more deeply teachers know their students. Consider how much easier it is to support students when you know what is challenging for them, to help students befriend each other when you know what they are interested in, and to involve students when you know their cultural social norms.

A challenging aspect of this dimension is that it takes time and intentionality for teachers to truly get to know their students. This is especially true for secondary teachers, who often have 150 or more students per year in their classroom. That's not an excuse; it just means that secondary teachers must work a little differently than their elementary colleagues and give themselves a bit more time to find success.

It's useful to remember that helping students feel known can be an evolving process. Students' identities may evolve over time as they grow. Hobbies or interests may change and become replaced by new ones. New friendships and talents may be formed. All of this affects the ways a teacher promotes alignment of the learners' self-views with how they are viewed by others.

Using a strengths-based approach can help students develop confidence and efficacious behaviors that result in academic achievement.[2] It is essential to know students as individuals rather than to speak about them in generalizations to avoid labeling students. Labels tend to focus on weaknesses or limitations ("autistic," "aggressive," or "shy") and can lead to false stereotypes and biases that can affect the quality, rigor, and equity of instruction that teachers provide to their students.

HOW DO WE GET TO KNOW STUDENTS PERSONALLY AND FOR THE STRENGTHS THEY POSSESS?

Indicators: Teachers described these indicators of a classroom and school environment where every student is known. Use these indicators to assess your own environment.

Table 5.1 • What Being Known Looks, Sounds, and Feels Like

What Does It Look Like?	What Does It Sound Like?	What Does It Feel Like?
• Modeling growth mindset	• Initiating the conversation	• Comfortable
• Building relationships	• Engaging in emotional responses	• Safe and secure
• Knowing deeper personal information	• Engaging in positive dialogue	• Reassured
• Having open and honest conversations	• Engaging in authentic conversations between students and teacher	• Celebrated as an individual by students and adults
• Conducting social-emotional check-ins	• Addressing biased and stereotyped language	• Respected
• Using engaged and relaxed body language	• Utilizing strengths and asset-based language	
• Students sitting with new people at lunch		
• Implementing "get-to-know-you" activities at the beginning of the school year, semester, and quarter		

TWO TRUTHS AND A LIE

Two of these statements are true; one is false. Can you spot the lie?

1. Knowing their own strengths helps students understand the perspectives of others.

2. If a teacher does not feel confident in how to address a biased or harmful comment or a behavior, it is better for them to avoid the situation or move past it without addressing it. It is better to not say anything than to say something "wrong."

3. When teachers effectively and intentionally use what they know about their students during instruction, they can build up students' strengths and help them make meaningful connections to themselves and their learning.

For students to convey who they are, they must first know themselves. This looks different depending on students' ages. Generally, there are several ways that people know and can define themselves, forming the acronym VIITALS:[3]

- **Values:** What drive us to make decisions in our lives and set goals, such as health or honesty

- **Identities:** Our race, ethnicity, religion, family/caregiver structure, socioeconomic status, sexual orientation, gender identity, and other characteristics or experiences that define who we are and how we experience the world around us

- **Interests:** Things that hold our attention over a sustained amount of time, including hobbies and passions

(Continued)

(Continued)

- **Temperament:** The personality traits or preferences we were born with (e.g., Are you detail-oriented or more of a big-picture person? Are you introverted or extroverted?)

- **Around-the-Clock Activities:** Our biorhythm—when we find ourselves with the most energy to accomplish things or engage in meaningful tasks (e.g., Are you most energized in the morning or late at night? Do you prefer to eat three meals, or are you less hungry in the morning and eat more later in the day?)

- **Life Mission and Meaningful Goals:** Knowing our purpose and where we derive meaning for ourselves, which develops over time through life experiences and can even change as a result of things like the death of a loved one, an illness, or a significant event

- **Strengths:** Our outward talents, abilities, and skills as well as our inner strengths

We can help students develop their VIITALS through purposeful activities and meaningful instruction. These activities can be simple, such as get-to-know-you lessons or learning preference inventories, or more in-depth through student debate of social justice topics or interest-driven research projects.[4] As we learn more about our students, we can use the information to help encourage meaningful relationships within the classroom, or we can strategically use interests to drive content instruction.[5]

Thus, the lie is the second statement. We may make mistakes in the way we address a situation, but rather than dwell on it, we can reframe it. Mistakes are opportunities for growth. Let's think about the situation in terms of academics. In math, when we are worried we'll make a procedural mistake, we don't just walk away from the problem and avoid solving it. We try our best and learn from our mistakes. The same is true for a situation where stereotypes, biased comments, or otherwise harmful language or actions occur. We should address the situation in the best way we know how. If later we realize we should have addressed the situation in a different way, then we should bring the group of students back together to acknowledge the mistake and rediscuss the situation. Avoiding the conversation altogether dismisses and devalues those harmed by the comment or situation, and it gives a silent message to the student(s) who did harm that their actions or words are acceptable.[6]

UTILIZE A STRENGTHS-BASED APPROACH

We only have ourselves to blame. The educational field is infused with beliefs and practices that are designed to surface student learning difficulties and address them. But the unintended result can be that in our zeal to identify what students cannot do, our attention constricts. Think about how many data team meetings you've been to that focused only on data about what the students could *not* do.

There is another way. Instead of focusing on what students cannot do, we can seek to locate strengths in equal measure using a strengths-based approach. There's one simple rule: Shine a spotlight on what students do well. That does not mean that we ignore areas of growth, but rather that we build on what students can already do and then make our plans based on what they will be able to do with support. The evidence suggests that focusing on strengths produces greater levels of happiness and engagement at school and higher levels of academic achievement overall.[7]

Table 5.2 • What a Strengths-Based Approach Is and Is Not

A Strengths-Based Approach Is . . .	A Strengths-Based Approach Is *Not* . . .
• Valuing everyone equally and focusing on what the child can do rather than what the child cannot do • Describing learning and development respectfully and honestly • Building on a child's abilities within their zone of proximal and potential development	• Only about "positive" things • A way of avoiding the truth • About accommodating bad behavior • Fixating on problems • About minimizing concerns • One-sided • A tool to label individuals

(Continued)

(Continued)

A Strengths-Based Approach Is . . .	A Strengths-Based Approach Is *Not* . . .
• Acknowledging that people experience difficulties and challenges that need attention and support • Identifying what is taking place when learning and development go well, so that it may be reproduced, further developed, and strengthened	

Source: Victoria Department of Education and Early Childhood Development (2012).

A teacher's commitment to a strengths-based approach promotes students' own self-awareness about their traits, identities, and characteristics. Identifying students' strengths allows learners to leverage assets, while acknowledging the opportunities to advance the skills they might be still developing. There is good evidence that self-knowledge—which is to say knowing, naming, and leveraging personal strengths—contributes significantly to confidence, life satisfaction, and the quality of personal and professional relationships.[8] This is especially important for students at risk of being marginalized. As one example, a study of Black junior high school students (grades 7–9) who reported a higher degree of personal strengths and cultural assets demonstrated higher rates of academic persistence (e.g., "If I can't get a problem right the first time, I just keep trying").[9]

We are fans of a series of questions that can be used in teacher team meetings or during a parent/caregiver-teacher conference to ensure that we are using a strengths-based approach.[10] Some sample questions include the following:

1. This student excels at . . .

2. This student has an amazing ability to . . .

3. This student is frequently recognized for . . .

4. This student smiles when . . .

5. This student is happiest when . . .

6. This student participates the most when . . .

7. This student is highly interested in . . .

8. This student is highly motivated by . . .

9. This student always takes pride in their work when . . .

10. This student enjoys talking about . . .

TAKE ACTION

Identify a hard-to-reach, hard-to-teach student. It's easy to talk about a strengths-based approach in a theoretical way, but it's more challenging when we're talking about "that kid." (You know, the one who keeps you awake at night as you struggle to make a breakthrough. That child who frustrates you. That young person who causes you to dread third period because you know they came to school today.) Now that you've got that current student in your mind, ask yourself the questions presented a moment ago. We like to think of these students as simply hard-to-reach or hard-to-teach. The reframing is important because it places the responsibility back on us: caring adults who have the potential to do something about it.

Make a plan to get information about the questions you can't answer. It's likely there were at least one or two questions about the student that you weren't able to answer. How might you get the information you need? Consider discussions you might have with the learner or their family/caregivers to get a better portrait of the young person so that you can confidently respond to each of the questions.

QUICK START

	I can start this tomorrow!	I can begin this month	I need to discuss this with others	Resources needed
When providing feedback, ask the student to identify something they did well or are proud of.				
Use strengths-based language in instruction (e.g., "This next item is hard, but we have the knowledge to be successful together.")				
Spotlight students for their strengths (e.g., "I'm glad Jessenia is here because she knows so much about this topic.")				

PERSONAL BEST GOALS

Build the habits of a strength-based approach and you'll open the door to individualized goal setting for students who are not yet making expected progress. Students who are facing a gap in their learning can become discouraged when they compare themselves to other classmates. Outside the classroom, personal best goals are goals that people of all ages and circumstances develop to compare their own performance to earlier efforts. If you are a runner, for instance, one of the measures of improvement is the "personal record" (or PR). The gauge isn't limited to competition with others. The PR lets runners measure their own improvement.

In the classroom, personal best goals can be academic goals for the completion of coursework. These goals should be easily measured and bound in time. In addition, they meet the following four conditions:[11]

- Specific in nature
- Challenging to the student
- Competitively self-referenced
- Based on self-improvement

These growth-oriented goals are set by the student to improve on previous performance. Don't miss this important element—these are goals *set by the student*, not by someone else. They can be outcome goals, such as "I will improve my comprehension skills so I can achieve a new benchmark in my reading level," or process-oriented, such as "I will read for fifteen minutes every evening."

Notice that neither of these goals involves comparisons to others; personal best goals are progress-oriented. Because the goal is co-constructed with the student, personal best goals are associated with higher levels of intrinsic motivation, persistence, engagement, and enjoyment of school.[12] Goals set with students can be personal (e.g., trying out for the swim team) or nonacademic but school related (e.g., improving attendance). Goals should challenge the student yet be reachable. The effect size of appropriately challenging goals is 0.59.

Strengthen students' personal link to the goal by discussing why it is of value to them. Too often young people will go through a goal-setting exercise because there is an adult insisting on it. When you talk with them about why it is important to them (not to their school, family/caregivers, or friends), you further foster their sense of agency about the decisions they make and the direction they choose.

Don't get discouraged if their initial goals don't seem all that substantial. You are building a habit and a disposition for them. Regaining personal agency takes time, and it also takes early and small wins. Use a form like the one on the following page as a planning tool to hold a personal best conference with individual students.

Figure 5.1 · Conference Planning Tool

What is an academic, school-related, or personal goal you have for yourself?

- Why is this something you value?
- What has your past performance been like? What has been your personal best so far?
- How will you know you have been successful?
- What might get in the way of you meeting this goal?
- What do you need to achieve this goal?

Resources	Self	School	Family/Caregivers

Action steps to achieve this goal:

1.
2.
3.

We will check in with each other every _____ weeks to talk about your progress toward your personal best goal.

online resources Available for download at **resources.corwin.com/belongingplaybook**

TAKE ACTION

Revisit personal best goals regularly with students. Importantly, it isn't so much the initial goal setting that has an effect, but rather what is done with it. If a goal is set but never revisited, it holds little to no value and the student may feel dismissed. Check in regularly with students to discuss their progress and adjust their planned actions as needed. Knowing that their plans can be adjusted based on new circumstances can be an eye-opener for students.

Share goals you have for yourself currently and how you're working toward them. Students often look at the adults in their lives and see the accomplishments—but not all the zigzags it took to get there. They'll never know how you are using knowledge of your own strengths and the supports you need if all they see are the outcomes, not the path you are taking to get there.

QUICK START

	I can start this tomorrow!	I can begin this month	I need to discuss this with others	Resources needed
Share a current goal you have with students and what you are doing to achieve it.				
Highlight examples in stories when a character sets a goal.				
Identify students in your classroom who would benefit from setting personal best goals.				

STEREOTYPE THREAT AND MINDSET

Stereotype threat is the worry that your behavior or performance will confirm negative stereotypes held about your group or affiliation.[13] Once evoked, the anxiety about the stereotype negatively impacts performance on tasks. First identified with Black students on test performance, it has since been demonstrated in girls in advanced math and science courses, as well as children of migrant farmworkers, unhoused students, students with disabilities, LGBTQIA+ learners, Latino/x/e students, Indigenous students, and other people of color. The fear of being judged negatively can have a profound effect on learning,[14] with an effect size of −0.29, meaning that it can cause an actual reversal of learning.[15]

The feeling of stereotype threat can be further amplified in situations where biased comments, slurs, hate speech, microaggressions, or bullying occurs. The majority of these are related to race, religion, sexual orientation, and gender identity and gender expression. Addressing this kind of behavior is not always easy. It can feel uncomfortable or scary. But speaking up and pausing instruction to address the situation is necessary to ensure all students feel known for who they really are and to advance their sense of belonging in your classroom. When teachers confront biased thinking, it chips away at student misconceptions, decreases bullying behavior, promotes kindness and respect, and prepares learners for a successful future in our diverse world. Equally important, it indicates to students who were harmed that their identities are of value and that they matter.

Stereotype threat can turn inward too. Internalized messages can lead to students developing a fixed mindset about their capacity to learn and thrive. Carol Dweck introduced the concepts of fixed and growth mindset as a way to explain how we respond to failure.[16] A person with a fixed mindset about a situation fears that the failure will expose a weakness they have to others. On the other hand, a person with a growth mindset sees the failure as something they can positively impact through their efforts. Mindsets are not monolithic: We all have varying mindsets depending on whether the situation is academic, athletic, social, or creative.

Our goal as teachers is to shape the mindsets of our students so that they feel confident about who they are and can witness the powerful effect of their own efforts. To do so requires that we ensure that our classrooms are places where all students are identity-safe[17] and all learners get to see how their efforts deliver results. These examples, from the American University School of Education, compare and contrast how the language shifts of teachers can make a difference in how students view their learning efforts.[18]

Statements about the learning process:

- Fixed mindset statement: "It's OK if you're having trouble. Maybe algebra isn't one of your strengths."

- Growth mindset statement: "When you learn how to do a new kind of problem, it develops your math brain."

Encouraging students to work through problems:

- Fixed mindset statement: "Great effort. You tried as hard as you could."

- Growth mindset statement: "The goal isn't to get it right immediately. The goal is to improve your understanding step by step. What can you try next?"

Encouraging students when they experience difficulty:

- Fixed mindset statement: "Don't worry, you'll get it if you keep trying."

- Growth mindset statement: "That feeling you're experiencing of algebra being hard is the feeling of your brain developing."

TAKE ACTION

Use growth-producing language in verbal and written feedback. Develop the habit of providing feedback about effort and normalize struggle as part of the learning process. At the same time, let learners know about the high expectations you have for them and your willingness to support their efforts. Make sure they understand that they don't need to go it alone.

Provide opportunities for students to learn about the struggles of others. Feeling known requires that students believe their traits, identities, and characteristics are understood by others. Too often, students incorrectly believe that learning is easy for others but hard for themselves. Host discussions with students in advance of tests and major projects. Invite students to share what is currently difficult for them and ask them about the actions they are taking.

Emphasize students' strengths. By consistently affirming each student's strengths (e.g., hard-working, organized, talented, determined), teachers can reframe gender, cultural, identity, or racial stereotypes that may exist.

Address negative comments swiftly. Young people sometimes say things that are thoughtless, hurtful, and harmful. When negative comments are made in the classroom, address them immediately. Be sure to discuss it with the person who made the comment, as well as those who were harmed. When harmful statements are not addressed, they are perceived by students as being a tacit acceptance of the sentiment on your part.

QUICK START

	I can start this tomorrow!	I can begin this month	I need to discuss this with others	Resources needed
Discuss with grade or subject colleagues potential stereotype threats that may exist for your students.				
Provide examples of the achievement of people who share similar identities with your students.				
Use the power of *yet* in your language: "We haven't mastered this *yet*, but we will."				

CASE IN POINT: FEELING KNOWN AND KNOWING OTHERS

At the beginning of the school year, Pablo Chavez was excited to get to know his new group of seventh graders. At the start of each period, he gave each of his students a blank paper puzzle piece. He explained to the students that each of them would have the opportunity to decorate their piece with words, symbols, or drawings that represent them. He made a point to invite students to share as much as they were comfortable with, and he acknowledged that it's okay to keep some information private.

To help students feel more comfortable, Mr. Chavez made his piece ahead of time, and he decided to share what he had created before the students began to work on their own. Mr. Chavez intentionally shared mostly surface-level information (e.g., his favorite foods and people in his family), but he also shared some deeper personal information about his fear of spiders (in the form of a drawing of the spider with a big red X through it), and how he was the first person in his family to graduate from college (represented by a drawing of a graduation cap).

Mr. Chavez then displayed some categories of information that students could use to think about the different things they might want to share about themselves. The categories included favorites (e.g., music, food, movie, color, book), family/caregivers, important identities, hobbies and passions, skills, likes and dislikes, future aspirations, fears, and pet peeves.

Once students were finished with their puzzle pieces, he had them place their puzzle pieces on their desks and then do a gallery walk around the classroom to look at everyone else's creations. He encouraged students to note others whom they might share similarities with or whom they had questions for. When everyone had finished sharing, he collected the puzzle pieces and then fit them together into one large puzzle on the wall of his classroom. It symbolized how each person in the class was unique, but together they formed one classroom community.

What's Your Advice?

- This can be a good activity for the start of the year, but its potential is wasted if Mr. Chavez never revisits it. What are three suggestions you can give the teacher for how to use what he has learned throughout the year?

- List three suggestions that could help Mr. Chavez ensure that his students learn more about their classmates throughout the year.

WHAT'S NEXT?

ESSENTIAL QUESTION

How do we get to know students personally and for the strengths they possess?

THINK ABOUT

- How are students in your classroom learning about themselves and their peers so that they feel confident in who they are, and that they feel known (and valued) by others?

- Is there a disposition to discussing a strengths-based approach for students in meetings with other adults? If not, how can you shift this disposition?

- What are the stereotype threats students in your class or subject area are most vulnerable to? What steps do you take to interrupt this anxiety?

- What resources and professional learning do you need to continue to build your cultural competency?

START – STOP – KEEP

Based on what you learned in this module, answer the questions that follow.

Start: What practice(s) would you like to start doing?
Stop: What practice(s) would you like to stop doing?
Keep: What practice(s) would you like to keep doing?

6 SUPPORTED

Support comes in many forms, from academic to emotional, and from different people—including peers and teachers. When we feel that we belong, we accept support from others. In fact, we come to expect that support will be provided because the environment is safe enough for us to be vulnerable and share our needs with others. As Brené Brown reminds us, "Vulnerability is the birthplace of innovation, creativity, and change."[1]

When it comes to academic support, most educators recognize the value of focusing on students' zone of proximal development, a theory that was first articulated by Russian developmental psychologist Lev Vygotsky in the 1920s but did not become well known until his work was translated decades later.[2] To be supported means that learners regularly experience this zone of proximal development, which requires that someone else handle the tricky parts as the student is learning. In educational language, this is known as scaffolding and there are specific actions that teachers and peers can take to provide this type of support.

But being supported also means that teachers understand that there is also a zone of potential development and that, with appropriate support, students will reach greater and greater success. Beyond scaffolding, this type of support is provided in the design of meaningful learning experiences, or lesson design as it is known in the Visible Learning database. With an effect size of 0.70, there are specific actions teachers can take to support students learning in the lessons they create.

In addition to academic support, teachers and peers provide emotional support. This allows students to learn to regulate their emotions and the associated behaviors, which are part of emotional intelligence. Emotional intelligence has an effect size of 0.63 and supports students' academic learning as well. This can include daily check-ins, creating a culture of kindness, or creating spaces for students to calm down. When students feel supported emotionally, they are much more likely to engage in self-regulation and learn more.

HOW ARE WE PROVIDING THE ASSISTANCE ALL STUDENTS NEED TO PARTICIPATE FULLY AND MEANINGFULLY?

Indicators: Teachers described these indicators of a classroom and school environment where students feel supported academically and emotionally. Use these indicators to assess your own environment.

Table 6.1 • What Being Supported Looks, Sounds, and Feels Like

What Does It Look Like?	What Does It Sound Like?	What Does It Feel Like?
• Providing language frames to scaffold discussion and writing • Creating and referencing student goals often • Referring to support resources • Holding and communicating high expectations for all students • Modeling and demonstrating new learning tasks • Students taking risks without fear of judgment • Ensuring that the physical environment is student-centered	• Students asking for help • Students accepting help or politely declining help • Teachers and students offering help and assistance • Teachers prompting and cueing using affirmations • Having restorative conversations (peer to peer or teacher to student)	• Valued • Safe • Empowered • Shielded

TWO TRUTHS AND A LIE

Two of these statements are true; one is false. Can you spot the lie?

1. Reading firsthand accounts from older peers about shared academic or social worries can decrease worry and help improve grades for students transitioning to middle school.

2. Trauma-sensitive schools seek to proactively build in supports for students on the assumption that schools do not always know which students have experienced trauma.

3. Teacher subject-matter knowledge is strongly associated with student academic outcomes.

It's amazing to think that simply addressing head-on worries about belonging can make a positive difference, but that's what researchers discovered in a brief intervention with incoming middle school students.[3] The students completed two reading and writing assignments in the first and third months of school. These consisted of first-person vignettes by older students who initially felt "belonging uncertainty" (anxiety of being unsure about their place in an environment). The researchers tracked student progress and found that compared to a control group, their grade point averages rose and course failures decreased.

Delivering support proactively means that you don't wait to find out who is experiencing a disconnection with school. You assume that everyone might benefit. Trauma-sensitive schools rest on the assumption that supports should be proactively designed to mitigate undiagnosed trauma.[4] Therefore, there is attention to offering consistent structures, routines, and procedures to provide a safe and supportive classroom. There is continued outreach to—and communication with—families/caregivers. Most importantly, there are ongoing efforts to establish and maintain positive relationships among students and teachers.

The lie? Believing that simply knowing the subject matter is sufficient. While important on its own, knowing subject matter has an effect size of 0.13 in terms of student achievement.[5] Understanding pedagogy and instruction matters deeply. Knowing something and knowing how to teach something are two different somethings.

QUALITY INSTRUCTION AND SCAFFOLDING

Students spend thousands of hours with teachers over the course of their K–12 education, and they come to know what it feels like to be supported in their learning. When teachers provide high-quality learning experiences, students develop skills and concepts. There should be a direct relationship between the teaching that occurs and the learning that results. If students are not learning, then teachers need to change the instruction. We can never hold an instructional strategy in higher esteem than our students' learning. In general, students need to have ideas and information explained, have their errors addressed, be provided opportunities to collaborate with peers, and be held accountable to practice and apply what they have learned.

High-quality instruction involves the use of research-based instructional practices to promote rigor, collaboration, and engagement with standards-based content. Students should have equitable access to both content and materials to support their learning needs. One way to ensure access is through the use of scaffolding. However, when teachers over-scaffold, rigor is reduced, and students become dependent on the teacher. Student dependency has a negative impact on learning, with an effect size of −0.24. When appropriately used, scaffolding has a positive impact, with an effect size of 0.58. Here are two types of scaffolds:[6]

- *Just-in-case scaffolds* are provided to all students just in case they need them for learning.

- *Just-in-time scaffolds* are provided at the point of use, only to students who have demonstrated a need.

TAKE ACTION

Model and demonstrate often. Students need examples of what they will eventually accomplish on their own. Show students how you use concepts, skills, and strategies, and think aloud so that students witness the thinking and can apply it on their own. Modeling can also include non-examples with strengths and error analysis as well as opportunities for revision and reflection.

Guide students' thinking. Create a climate in which mistakes are celebrated as opportunities to learn. Try not to tell students what to think or what the answers are, as this could lead to learned helplessness. Instead, use prompts and cues to address errors and mistakes. Prompts are actions that encourage something to happen in the learners' mind, whereas cues are hints that provide students with information about where to pay attention.

Create collaboration opportunities. Belonging is fostered when students have productive opportunities to collaborate with their peers. However, belonging can be thwarted when one student does all the work for the group. Build in accountability measures for each student and their contribution to the group.

Assign independent tasks, both in class and outside of class. Independent tasks should involve undertakings that you are fairly certain students can do on their own. These tasks should provide students an opportunity to practice what they have learned and then apply that learning in new situations.

Consider when to scaffold. Although it is common practice to provide scaffolds for all students in advance of the lesson, the supports enacted should be distributed across the learning tasks, and they should be intentionally faded as students acquire knowledge and skills.

QUICK START

	I can start this tomorrow!	I can begin this month	I need to discuss this with others	Resources needed
Inventory the instructional routines used in class, with attention to peer collaboration and belonging.				
Log the scaffolds that are provided to students. Which of them are just-in-case versus just-in-time?				
Make a plan to fade some scaffolds.				

TRAUMA-SENSITIVE CLASSROOM DESIGN

JUMPY

ANXIOUS

WORRIED

SOCIALLY WITHDRAWN

CAN'T FOCUS

FAST, SHALLOW BREATHING

EASILY STARTLED

EASILY ANGERED

The toll trauma takes on learning is staggering. Thankfully, educators around the world are learning about the impact that trauma has on children and youth, and they are working hard to create trauma-sensitive practices that address the needs of students with these experiences. Educators are building healthy, growth-producing relationships; giving supportive feedback to reduce negative thinking; providing increased predictability; and fostering a sense of safety in the classroom.[7]

Many students who have experienced trauma are hypervigilant, meaning they are in a heightened state of alert. It is the brain's way of protecting us from harm. When it comes to learning, this heightened state of alert can distract students because they are concerned about possible threats. Their outward behaviors—such as appearing to not pay attention to instruction or looking around the room—are often misinterpreted by teachers as problematic behavior. Even the physical environment of the classroom can unintentionally contribute to a student's need to remain hypervigilant.

Designs 4 Dignity (D4D) is a pro bono design firm that helps nonprofits that work with vulnerable populations to create physical spaces that are restorative.[8] They recognized that the physical environment can intensify negative experiences of people who have been traumatized. D4D's work is shaped by the principles of trauma-informed design outlined by the Committee on Temporary Shelter, as listed here:[9]

- *Realize* how the physical environment affects an individual's sense of identity, worth, dignity, and empowerment;

- *Recognize* that the physical environment has an impact on attitude, mood, and behavior, and that there is a strong link between our physiological state, our emotional state, and the physical environment; and

- *Respond* by designing and maintaining supportive and healing environments for trauma-experienced residents.

As we work toward supporting students, let's make sure our efforts are not thwarted by the physical design of learning spaces.

TAKE ACTION

Examine the spatial layout. Look at sightlines from multiple seated areas in your classroom. Hypervigilant students often have a strong need to see the classroom windows and especially the doors so they can watch who is coming and going. Avoid placing chairs that require students to have their back to the door.

Perform a color check. Color has an influence on mood. Deeply saturated colors, especially warm colors like red, orange, and yellow, can provoke anxiousness. Lighter shades of blue, purple, and green are calming colors. While you may not be able to choose the color of your walls, you can eliminate the bright neon paper decorations that are so popular in many classrooms.

Assess noise and light levels. The amplifying effect of so many hard surfaces can create a jarring acoustic environment. Carpet absorbs sound and can lower sharper sounds. If you are able, use carpet tiles (which are easily replaced when damaged). If not, consider using carpet runners in high-traffic areas. Natural light from windows as well as light from environmentally friendly LED lights is far better than the flicker of fluorescent lighting.

QUICK START

	I can start this tomorrow!	I can begin this month	I need to discuss this with others	Resources needed
Reduce clutter, because a disorganized classroom makes everyone more anxious.				
Get rid of the hanging stuff, because overhead objects can feel oppressive to hypervigilant people.				
Add a pop of nature. A plant, a water feature, or even pictures of nature can contribute to a calming atmosphere.				

SELF-AFFIRMATION INTERVENTIONS

Self-affirmations are situational opportunities, often brief in nature, that allow people to affirm their global self-integrity.[10] This theory, developed by Claude Steele (who also identified stereotype threat as a phenomenon), suggests that people generally want to maintain an image of themselves as "morally and adaptively adequate."[11] In other words, we want to see ourselves as good people who are able to control important outcomes in our lives.

In many social situations, our self-integrity—the quality of being truthful and honest with ourselves and others while aligning our behaviors with our values—is threatened. When that happens, our growth and development are impeded. In contrast, when self-integrity and affirmations occur, our performance increases, and the benefits have been shown to persist for several years.[12]

There have been several studies about actions that educators can take to integrate self-affirmations into the curriculum. For example, having students engage in reflective writing that affirms their values improves their academic performance. These writing tasks allow students to reflect on core values, "assuring them of their belonging in school, by highlighting the personal relevance of academic coursework, or by cultivating the belief that intelligence is malleable rather than fixed."[13]

Typically, teachers introduce self-affirmation writing exercises by providing students with a list of values and asking learners to choose a few that are of interest to them. Students then write a brief essay in which they explain why the values are important to them and share times or situations when those values were important. These essays are not generic because "a key aspect of the affirmation intervention is that its content is self-generated and tailored to tap into each person's particular valued identity."[14] A middle schooler from the intervention study wrote,

> Dance is important to me, because it is my passion, my life. My second home is the dance studio, my second family is my dance team. My family and friends are so important to me, even more than dance. My family, I can't live without them. My friends, I am my real self around them (and my sister). I can be silly, goofy, and weird and they don't care, they accept me for who I am. . . . And for being creative, I LOVE being creative in dance. When I'm dancing or making a dance it takes me to another place.[15]

The evidence suggests that self-affirmation interventions work because they do two things:

- *Buffer against threat.* These affirmations assure people that they can rally their personal resources to address the demands of the task or the adversity they face.

- *Reduce defensiveness.* These affirmations also provide a protective layer over people's sense of threat and reduce the likelihood that they respond in defensive ways when they perceive a threat.

These self-affirmations are relatively simple to implement in the classroom, yet there is powerful and documented evidence of their impact. Ultimately, they foster belonging because they are a tangible support that students can use.

TAKE ACTION

Incorporate reflective writing or drawing. Regularly ask students to reflect on their values and interests, such as music, athletics, creativity, connections with others, sense of humor, and the like. Ask students to identify why these values and interests are important, to provide examples of when the values and interests served as a resource, and to describe what the values and interests mean to them. Younger students can draw images of their values and interests and share orally.

(Continued)

(Continued)

Focus on values before stressful events. When students focus on their values before stressful events, they tend to do better. For example, consider a major public performance task, such as a presentation or public speaking. Rather than focusing on the task itself, self-affirmation interventions suggest that focusing on what an individual values helps them rally their resources to do well. A student who values kindness and personal relationships may see their performance on a stressful public speaking assignment differently after their reflection because they want to maintain the relations with peers in the class.

Consider digital self-affirmation tasks. Consider asking older students who are active users of social media to engage in self-affirmation tasks outside of the school day via online tools.[16] For example, using a messaging service such as Remind, SchoolMessenger, ParentSquare, or BrightArrow, teachers can send a prompt asking students to reflect on the values they identified as important during a class activity. The students respond with a single sentence about why this value is important to them, either using the messaging system or in their learning management system.

QUICK START

	I can start this tomorrow!	I can begin this month	I need to discuss this with others	Resources needed
Add reflective writing tasks about values to your lesson plan calendar (4–6 times per semester).				
During stressful academic or social times, remind students of their values and the reasons they hold these values.				
Use a weekly affirmation at the start of each lesson.				

CASE IN POINT: THE STUDENT STUDY TEAM

The Student Study Team (SST) at Casey Middle School convenes monthly to examine the academic, social, and behavioral progress of students of concern. The names of individual students can be submitted by parents/caregivers or teachers; this step is often performed before referring students for special education assessment. The SST at this school uses a multidisciplinary approach framed by four questions:

- What's the problem?

- Why is it occurring?

- What are we going to do about it?

- How is the student responding to the intervention?

One month, the team met to discuss Marlo, a seventh-grade student who had recently transferred from a neighboring district. She and her mother also attended the meeting. The team had received Marlo's records from her former school, which indicated that she was a good student who did not have any major behavioral concerns. However, during the past month Marlo had already been absent 12 percent of the days (all excused), was not completing work in her English and math classes (but her social studies and science grades were very good), and her teachers had observed that she seemed distracted.

What's Your Advice?

- What questions do you advise that the SST should pose?

- What other information do they need?

- What advice do you have about errors the SST should avoid?

WHAT'S NEXT?

ESSENTIAL QUESTION

How are we providing the assistance all students need to participate fully and meaningfully?

THINK ABOUT

- What is the evidence of success with existing support systems in your classroom or school?

- How do you innovate beyond existing support systems in your classroom or school?

- How can you more fully involve students and families/caregivers in developing support systems in your classroom or school?

START – STOP – KEEP

Based on what you learned in this module, answer the questions that follow.

Start: What practice(s) would you like to start doing?

Stop: What practice(s) would you like to stop doing?

Keep: What practice(s) would you like to keep doing?

7 BEFRIENDED

The importance of friendships throughout our lives cannot be overstated. During infancy, we form bonds with caregivers and close family, but soon relationships form with peers. In doing so, we learn much about ourselves and what it takes to form, maintain, and repair friendships. In fact, the effect size of friendships in school is 0.38, an important and inexpensive way to facilitate learning.

High-quality friendships provide young people with social provisions, which are the benefits derived from the relationship. Social provisions include "companionship, help, validation, and opportunities for self-disclosure."[1] But children spend most of their time in classrooms with a range of peers, not just their closest friends. Newer research is confirming the indirect benefits in provision-rich classrooms. These are defined as classrooms where

> class members receive help from a higher proportion of their classmates, share companionship with a higher proportion of their classmates, have their contributions validated by a higher proportion of their classmates, and exchange personal information about themselves with a higher proportion of their classmates.[2]

One study found that provision-rich classrooms "buffered the effects on loneliness for children individually receiving fewer provisions from classmates."[3] In other words, for children with fewer high-quality individual friendships, provision-rich classrooms lessened their sense of loneliness. Friendships among children cannot be mandated, but they can be facilitated. When we are intentional about making sure that there is fertile ground for friendships to blossom, we increase friendship possibilities and foster better learning.

HOW ARE WE CREATING OPPORTUNITIES FOR FRIENDSHIPS TO FORM AND DEEPEN?

Indicators: Teachers described these indicators of a classroom and school environment where friendship formation is promoted and supported. Use these indicators to assess your own environment.

Table 7.1 • **What Being Befriended Looks, Sounds, and Feels Like**

What Does It Look Like?	What Does It Sound Like?	What Does It Feel Like?
• Students having friendships inside and outside of school • Smiles • Students sitting together or playing together at lunch or recess • Students walking together around campus • Using friendly greetings and body language • Providing intentional support and guidance to build student friendships • Strategically grouping and pairing students for activities or discussion to encourage friendships	• Engaging conversations • Laughter and excitement • Asking for help • Using a positive tone • Showing patience and empathy • Thinking of the needs of others	• Safe to be vulnerable • Organic • Comfortable • Cozy • Agreeable

TWO TRUTHS AND A LIE

Two of these statements are true; one is false. Can you spot the lie?

1. Students in classrooms led by culturally competent teachers enjoy more cross-group friendships.
2. High-quality friendships are a protective factor against cyberbullying.
3. Childhood friendships have a limited influence on the health of older adults.

Students are more likely to form friendships with people who share the same racial, gender, linguistic, or ability characteristics. But this can put marginalized students in danger, as Beverly Tatum poignantly documented in *Why Are All the Black Kids Sitting Together in the Cafeteria?*[4] She and other scholars have long called out the institutional barriers that limit friendships across groups due to "othering," which sees other groups as inherently different and inferior due to unaddressed biases. But it turns out that teachers who scored highly on measures of cultural competence had classrooms where more cross-group friendships emerged.[5] Additionally, culturally responsive teaching has been shown to help students overcome their implicit biases about difference. Teachers matter when it comes to the formation of school friendships, because they have an influence over reducing barriers that otherwise get in the way.

Friendships, both across groups and within groups, offer a protective factor when it comes to cyberbullying.[6] There can be a reciprocal effect of cyberbullying in that the student displaying bullying behavior and the student being bullied can be somewhat more fluid as the encounters go back and forth. Students who cyberbully on social media often have poor peer relationships, and they lash out at others. This behavior can lead to more problematic peer relationships. Further, the student who was bullied may become hostile and begin to display bullying behavior, too, thus perpetuating the cycle.[7] Having high-quality friendships reduces the frequency and severity of bullying behavior in schools.

The lie? The "long arm of childhood" extends the influence of school-aged friendships across the life span.[8] A study of adults over age forty-five found a correlation between positive childhood friendships and cognition, cognitive decline, and mental health in middle and late adulthood. Unfortunately, some teachers do not believe that it is their responsibility to foster friendships.

CLASSROOM SOCIOGRAMS

Think of a great class you have had in the past. Chances are that one of the reasons you immediately recalled the group was because of the positive ways they interacted with one another. Perhaps they looked out for one another or rallied around a classmate dealing with a difficult event in their life. You may have witnessed a higher degree of acceptance within the group for each classmate compared to other years. It was a provision-rich classroom, and everyone benefited.

That phenomenon has a name: *social cohesion*. The ability of a group to form positive relationships from within, while maintaining a sense of connection with the community, is fundamental to societies but also to smaller long-term groups like classrooms. Socially cohesive groups have a sense of solidarity. Social cohesion also has the potential to positively influence the learning of the group. With an effect size of 0.72, strong social cohesion can accelerate learning.

It works the other way too. The absence of social cohesion in the room may be due to implicit (or unaddressed) biases about differences, including race, ethnicity, religion, gender, sexual orientation, disability, family/caregiver structure, and linguistic diversity, among others. Understanding these relationships can provide insight into ways to broaden the social and emotional skills of students and their ability to view diversity as an asset to their learning. Creating a social map of the interactions of students can help you identify students who may be marginalized so you can take action.

A sociogram is a visual map of the network of relationships among the students in your classroom. Sociograms rely on the perceptions of students, not adults. Student reports of the dynamics between peers tend to be more accurate than teachers' or parents' perceptions as early as preschool.[9] Some children face peer rejection, often due to difficult behavior and aggressiveness. These students are especially vulnerable to experiencing a lower degree of academic achievement, isolation, and psychosocial maladjustment.[10] Identifying the peer-acceptance and peer-rejection dynamics occurring right under the surface provides teachers with ways to dismantle labels children give to one another, including misconceptions and implicit biases they have about differences.

TAKE ACTION

Develop a social map of your classroom. Administer a sociogram questionnaire a few weeks after the students in the class have had a chance to get to know one another. Explain to them that the questions are meant to help you get to know how they work best inside and outside the classroom. Ask students to confidentially answer the following questions:

- Who are three people in this class you would most like to play with at recess? (For older students, ask who they would like to eat lunch with.)

- Who are three people in this class you would most like to work with on a collaborative learning task?

- Who are three people in this class you would most like to meet with for a fun weekend activity?

Visualize the data. Once received, tally the number of times each student's name is cited, regardless of the type of interaction. For example, a student who is named twice for in-school social activities, once for academic tasks, and three times for out-of-school activities receives a score of 6. Organize the names in descending order from most frequently named to least frequently named. Place the names on a map like the one shown here, with the students named most often in the center square. Keep adding names to the concentric squares based on the number of times they were cited.

(Continued)

(Continued)

Figure 7.1 • Example Social Map

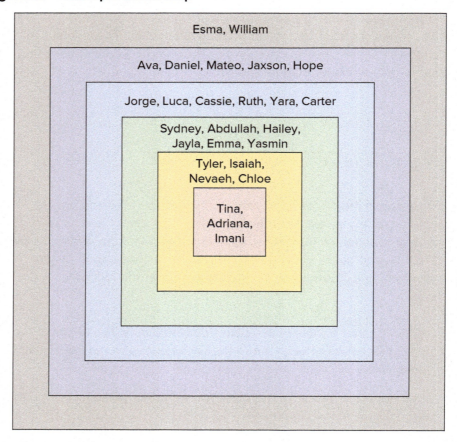

Esma, William

Ava, Daniel, Mateo, Jaxson, Hope

Jorge, Luca, Cassie, Ruth, Yara, Carter

Sydney, Abdullah, Hailey,
Jayla, Emma, Yasmin

Tyler, Isaiah,
Nevaeh, Chloe

Tina,
Adriana,
Imani

Analyze the data. The next step is to identify students who are outside the social network altogether. These are students who are not named by anyone. For instance, William and Esma do not appear to be connected. Observe these students and their interactions with peers to better understand possible barriers. These students can also benefit from positive attention from you. Sometimes students who exist on the margins of your classroom may not possess the prosocial skills that are helpful in developing friendships, or the cause could be something deeper, such as a safety concern. In these cases, efforts to help students to label emotions and solve problems, to learn how to seek support from a trusting adult, or to improve relationships with peers may be necessary.

QUICK START

	I can start this tomorrow!	I can begin this month	I need to discuss this with others	Resources needed
Notice students who do not seem befriended by others in the classroom.				
Identify actions you can take to reconnect that student to others or identify whether there are deeper issues, such as bullying.				
Use the alternate ranking system (Module 3) to group students to promote friendships.				

PEER-MEDIATED FRIENDSHIP INTERVENTIONS

It is not uncommon for students with disabilities, especially those with intellectual and developmental disabilities (IDD), to struggle to form and maintain friendships. This pattern in childhood sets the stage for adult outcomes regarding friendships. Among adults with IDD, 26 percent report having no friends who are not family members or paid staff.[11]

The emphasis on inclusive education has made friendships between students with and without disabilities more possible, at least in theory. But presence in a general education classroom alone is not sufficient when it comes to friendship formation. Recess and lunchtime can be especially fraught for students who have difficulty making friends, many of whom have autism spectrum disorder or other behavioral or communication difficulties. They can often be found eating on their own or seeking out a quiet part of the playground away from other children. Older students may go to the library or to a trusted teacher's room during lunch.

Moved by the isolation of some of her young students, kindergarten educator and scholar Vivian Paley made a new rule for her classroom: You can't say you can't play.[12] Throughout the year, she taught her young students how they could include others in their play activities. In doing so, she challenged the assumption that children are naturally cruel by appealing to their moral responsibility to each other.

The secret, however, is to make sure the friendships are peer-led. To be frank, well-meaning adults sometimes get in the way. The hovering presence of an adult can squelch the interactions. Adolescents are sensitive to the stigmatizing presence of an adult, who is perceived as monitoring their conversations. (Anyone who has driven a nearly silent car of teens home from an event knows what we mean.) Middle school students interviewed about their recommendations for fostering friendships with classmates with disabilities noted that "hang time" was important and need not always be about academics. One seemingly straightforward recommendation? "Let them ride the bus with us."[13]

One approach with demonstrably positive results is a peer-mediated intervention called Circle of Friends.[14,15] The intervention comes from a place of respect and consent. An identified student and their family/caregivers are fully involved in the process, beginning with the decision to pursue this intervention. Teachers identify three to six peers who might be interested in participating in the Circle of Friends. The overall purpose is to create a peer network for the focus child, with weekly thirty-minute meetings lasting for six to ten weeks.

The first meeting is conducted without the presence of the identified student, but with their knowledge and consent. The reason the focus student is not included in the first meeting is so that participating peers can speak about the child's strengths but also some of the difficulties they face in developing a relationship. Teachers can also provide information to peers about the student's disability, as well as their social and communication strengths and needs, to foster empathy and to solicit ideas about how to improve the situation. Their ideas are documented, and an implementation plan is made. As a follow-up, a teacher meets with the focus child and their family/caregivers to discuss the plan.

Subsequent weekly meetings are held with the focus child and their circle. They provide feedback to one another about successes and continued challenges, and they make plans for the following week. Their plans might include organized activities during class, meeting up at lunch or recess, or attending an afterschool club activity together. As the circle of friends becomes more comfortable with one another, the weekly meetings are faded out and attention is turned to how they can recruit other classmates to expand these strategies for daily use. This contributes to a more provision-rich classroom.

TAKE ACTION

Group formation. Observe the natural interactions that occur between the focus child and classmates. Consider recruiting these students into the circle. The students selected for the circle should have good social skills themselves. However, don't pressure reluctant students into participating, because it may be a forewarning of future negative interactions.

Monitor the intervention. Meetings should always be held with an adult to facilitate the conversation. Peers don't always know how to talk about sensitive subjects, and they may either self-silence or say something that is unintentionally hurtful.

Generalize the intervention. Make sure to leverage the successes experienced by the circle to expand into general classroom practices.

QUICK START

	I can start this tomorrow!	I can begin this month	I need to discuss this with others	Resources needed
Use what you have learned from your classroom sociogram to consider whether a peer-led friendship intervention is useful for the most marginalized of your students.				
Identify the circle of adults in the focus child's life and discuss the merits of a peer-led friendship intervention.				
Hold circles periodically to discuss issues related to friendship.				

BULLYING: RECOGNITION AND PREVENTION

As we noted in the opening of this module, students who have strong friendships are less likely to be bullied and are less likely to bully others. We are using the term *bullying* because we want to recognize that this is abusive and violent behavior against children and youth, and because of the research that has been conducted under this term.[16] The magnitude of the problem is staggering. On average, 22 percent of students are bullied each year on school property and 16 percent of teens report being cyberbullied at least once during the previous twelve months.[17] Middle school students, rural school students, and students identifying as two or more races are more often bullied.[18] The most common reasons for being bullied are physical appearance, gender identity, gender expression, sexual orientation, race or ethnicity, and political views.

Bullying impacts learning in significant ways academically, socially, and personally. The effect size of bullying on learning is −0.32. In other words, students who experience bullying learn less and even regress in their learning. Students who are bullied are at risk for depression, anxiety, sleep difficulties, and dropping out of school.[19]

It is also important to note that witnessing bullying behavior can have harmful effects on the school climate. Students who witness bullying at school are at higher risk for tobacco and drug use and mental health concerns.[20] Sadly, only about 20 percent of bullying incidents are reported. Students are reluctant to report because they fear being rejected, socially isolated, embarrassed and humiliated, or retaliated against. They are also concerned that they won't be believed or that educators won't effectively resolve the situation.[21]

Due to the significant harm bullying causes to all students, wise schools take a preventative approach to addressing bullying behavior. For example, schools can make a list of the common biases that tend to surface in the classroom or hallways, and then they can integrate antibias lessons to address them throughout the school year. Educators' commitment to preventing and stopping bullying has good effect. As one example, hate speech and hate-related graffiti at schools have been on a steady decline since 2009.[22]

The following chart contains signs that a student is being bullied or is bullying others. Since there is no method that prevents all bullying incidents, educators should be on the lookout for these signs and address bullying situations swiftly when they occur.[23]

Table 7.2 • Signs of Bullying

Signs a Student Is Being Bullied	Signs a Student Is Bullying Others
• Unexplainable injuries	• Gets into physical or verbal fights
• Lost or destroyed clothing, books, electronics, or jewelry	• Has friends who bully others
• Frequent headaches or stomachaches, feeling sick or faking illness	• Is increasingly aggressive
• Changes in eating habits, like suddenly skipping meals or binge eating (kids may come home from school hungry because they did not eat lunch)	• Gets sent to the principal's office or to detention frequently
	• Has unexplained extra money or new belongings
• Difficulty sleeping or frequent nightmares	• Blames others for their problems
• Declining grades, loss of interest in schoolwork, or not wanting to go to school	• Doesn't accept responsibility for their actions
• Sudden loss of friends or avoidance of social situations	• Is competitive and worries about their reputation or popularity
• Feelings of helplessness or decreased self-esteem	
• Self-destructive behaviors, such as running away from home, harming themselves, or talking about suicide	

TAKE ACTION

Help students understand bullying. When students know what bullying is, they can better identify it. Set clear expectations for actions students should take when bullying occurs, and be very open to these conversations. This approach signals to students that they can talk about bullying when they see it or when it happens to them. Your school and classroom should have clear expectations that include the prohibition of bullying and the harm bullying causes.

Teach students that there are many ways to be an upstander rather than a bystander. Teach students strategies for staying safe—offering tips such as using humor, saying "stop" directly and confidently, and walking away. These steps can help students take action immediately when they witness bullying.

Check in with students who are at risk or who have experienced bullying. Regular, brief conversations reassure students that they can share things if there is a problem. You can ask questions such as these:[24]

- What was one good thing that happened today? Any bad things?
- What was lunchtime like today? Who did you sit with? What did you talk about?
- What is it like to ride the school bus?
- What are you good at? What do you like best about yourself?

Encourage students to engage in their passions. When students participate in activities that they care about—including clubs, hobbies, and sports—they can build confidence, a bullying-protective factor.

Identify "gateway behaviors" for bullying. Often, bullying starts with some gateway behaviors that are not noticed or addressed. Some of these behaviors include eye rolling, prolonged staring, turning a back to a student, laughing cruelly or encouraging others to laugh, name calling, and ignoring or excluding others.[25]

Address bullying immediately. Given the academic and social impact of bullying, it's critical that educators respond swiftly and decisively when bullying occurs. In the classroom, teachers need to enforce anti-bullying rules. When you do notice these actions, tell the offender that *you* are offended rather than saying that the victim is or would be offended. Take the time to make a meaningful teachable moment and be sure that everyone who witnessed or heard the biased comment or bullying behavior hears you.

QUICK START

	I can start this tomorrow!	I can begin this month	I need to discuss this with others	Resources needed
Take note of gateway bullying behaviors that might be occurring in your classroom and make a plan to address them.				
Display school anti-bullying supports in your classroom and refer to them periodically.				
Advocate for professional learning on bullying prevention and how to effectively address implicit biases—especially about race, ethnicity, appearance, sexual orientation, and gender identity—because teachers may be unsure how to address them.				

CASE IN POINT: PROMOTING FRIENDSHIPS IN ELEMENTARY

Do you remember Mr. Green? He's the principal from Module 2's Case in Point who invited students with disabilities in his elementary school's boundary to attend their neighborhood school instead of the regional program.

After a few months, some of the new students were settling in well, but many others had difficulty in forming relationships with peers. Mr. Green recognized that being present is only the first step; these students might require more intensive supports. He pulled together a working committee consisting of general and special teachers, families/caregivers of students with disabilities, and the district special education director. He also developed a working agenda, with a reminder about maintaining the confidentiality of students:

- What's working well? What are the challenges?
- What do we know about friendship interventions?
- What do we still need to know?
- What resources do we need to be successful?

What's Your Advice?

- Imagine you are a member of this committee. Using what you know as a teacher, director, or family/caregiver of a person with a disability, what advice would you offer?
- What advice would you offer for a different student population (e.g., gifted or migrant)?

WHAT'S NEXT?

ESSENTIAL QUESTION

How are we creating opportunities for friendships to form and deepen?

THINK ABOUT

- In what ways is your classroom or school provision-rich? Where are the opportunities for growth?

- Are students' friendship opportunities viewed by staff as being outside of their job responsibilities?

- What is the status of bullying prevention efforts at your school? Is it "someone's job" or is it a shared effort for all the adults? How are students involved in bullying prevention?

START – STOP – KEEP

Based on what you learned in this module, answer the questions that follow.

Start: What practice(s) would you like to start doing?
Stop: What practice(s) would you like to stop doing?
Keep: What practice(s) would you like to keep doing?

NOTES

8

INVOLVED

As the opening quote implies, you can't get better at something by being a bystander. You have to actually practice and be involved in order to improve. You can watch online tutorial videos about how to play pickleball, but you won't ever be able to play the game yourself unless you pick up a racquet and get out on a court to practice. The same is true in the classroom. Students will not become independent problem solvers, develop critical-thinking skills, or collaborate well with others unless they become involved in their learning and take ownership of their academic success. In fact, research suggests that "granting students an active role in their learning can increase school completion; teach students valuable skills, like setting and attaining goals; and help students develop independence."[1]

When students are involved in their learning and in the function of the classroom, they will exhibit a variety of observable behaviors. You will see them ask each other questions, respond critically and respectfully to each other's comments, demonstrate active listening skills, and use each other as resources for learning. As they do so, their self-regulation skills are practiced and improved. The effect size of self-regulation on learning is 0.54. As a result of their increased self-regulation, students will be more actively engaged in lessons and participate in discussions. They will also be excited to set goals and achieve them. Ultimately, students build a higher sense of self-efficacy and begin to understand that learning is an ever-evolving process.

Table 8.1 • What Being Involved Looks, Sounds, and Feels Like

What Does It Look Like?	What Does It Sound Like?	What Does It Feel Like?
• Students engaging in learning outside the core classes • Students actively participating in class discussions • Actively seeking input from students • Students actively setting and pursuing common goals • Having students participate in the development of class norms and agreements • Students participating in opportunities outside of the classroom (sports, clubs) • Wearing spirit gear	• Using growth mindset language ("Start where you are. Use what you have. Do what you can.") • Having students actively participate in discussions and ask questions • Using developmentally appropriate and rigorous academic language • Allowing students to share their experiences and insights • Engaging in meaningful and collaborative conversations	• Important • Accountable • Confident • Excited to participate • Engaged • Proud • Equitable vulnerability • Complete • A valued member

TWO TRUTHS AND A LIE

Two of these statements are true; one is false. Can you spot the lie?

1. Significant planning and preparation are needed in order to involve students in the learning process.
2. Involving students in goals for their learning can improve academic motivation and achievement, promote social and emotional well-being, and increase engagement.
3. As students become more involved in their learning, they build self-reliance, better understand the tools they need for success, and are more willing to support others in their class.

Having goals is essential, but when students have little involvement in the development and monitoring of goals, they may be less successful. According to a meta-analysis of studies involving more than 15,000 students, taking a "person-centered approach" to goal construction can yield positive academic educational outcomes as well as foster emotional development.[2] This is further substantiated throughout Hattie's Visible Learning database, which indicates that learning works best "when teachers are able to see learning through the eyes of their students [and] students become their own teachers."[3] Their deep involvement in their learning—not just passive reception of teaching—is the gamechanger because it causes students to adopt the dispositions needed to learn.

Did you select the first statement as the lie? If you did, you're correct. While involving students in the learning process does include intentionality, planning, and preparation,[4] there are some simple ways to incorporate this dimension of belonging such that it builds students' self-efficacy and promotes academic success:

- **Give students roles and responsibilities.** When students share governance of the classroom, they are more engaged in the collective success of all learners. The classroom does not exclusively belong to the teacher; it is "owned" by the entire class, which promotes a sense of community and belonging.

- **Create clarity to support student ownership.** In order for students to take ownership of their learning, they must clearly understand what is expected. Learning targets and success criteria should be written in student-friendly language, so that students and teachers can set attainable academic learning goals. With clear expectations, students can monitor their progress and know when they are successful.

- **Allot more time for collaboration and active learning.** Students become more involved in their learning through tasks designed to explore concepts, collaborate with peers, and build critical thinking.

- **Incorporate opportunities for choice and decision-making.** Choice is an important tool that promotes self-reliance and decision-making skills. Using instructional strategies such as a choice board or a menu of options provides students with opportunities to choose academic tasks or activities to complete and puts ownership of success in their court, where it belongs.

BUILDING STUDENTS' SELF-EFFICACY

Self-efficacy is a person's particular set of beliefs that determine how well they can execute a plan of action in a variety of situations.[5] A student with high self-efficacy believes that they have the power to influence their actions, motivation, and environment enough to achieve success. Highly efficacious students also persist longer and devote the energy needed to achieve their goals, compared to students with a lower sense of self-efficacy. With an effect size of 0.67, the efficacy of a student has the potential to accelerate learning considerably.[6]

By focusing on self-efficacy, teachers create a classroom environment that cultivates belonging and involvement where students are more likely to feel safe and valued. Importantly, they are more willing to take academic risks and keep trying. The dispositions of being persistent and having the confidence to accept challenge paves the way for students to maximize their potential.[7]

For students, being involved in their learning and building self-efficacy go hand-in-hand. The more learners can set goals, take steps toward achieving them, and concretely monitor their progress, the more their self-efficacy increases. However, it is important for teachers to have a plan for when students experience challenges or setbacks in the pursuit of learning so that students do not backtrack in their self-efficacy and withdraw their involvement. Here are some ideas.[8]

Table 8.2 • Approaches Versus Expectations

Approach	Expectation
Set goals together.	One of the most effective ways of building student confidence is making sure everyone is on the same page about learning goals. There is value in having clear learning intentions and success criteria. To build confidence, students and tutors need to understand and agree on the goals for learning.
Encourage self-assessment.	A huge step toward building student confidence is in providing students opportunities to improve learning by encouraging ownership of this learning. When students learn to self-assess, the role of the teacher becomes to validate and challenge, rather than to decide whether the students have learned. When we do this, student understanding, ownership, enthusiasm for learning, and, of course, competence, increase.
Give useful feedback.	Feedback should make someone feel good about where they are and get them excited about where they can go. This is the exact mindset that develops as we continue building our learners' confidence in the classroom.
Empty their heads.	Students tend to lose confidence in themselves because they feel they're struggling more than they are. Every once in a while, we've got to get learners to unpack everything in their heads through review and open discussion to show them just how much they've accomplished.
Show that effort is normal.	Nothing kills confidence more than a student thinking they're the only one in class who doesn't understand something. Focus on the effort that everyone is making. A good way of building student confidence in such a case is by having that struggling student pair up with one of the others who has aced the topic and get them to explain it.
Celebrate success.	Any kind of success in learning, no matter how big or small, deserves to be acknowledged and celebrated. This might mean more to some students than to others, but it's still a great way of building student confidence.

TAKE ACTION

Incorporate "must-haves" and "amazings."[9] Think about an upcoming task or unit of study. Develop success criteria that include *must-haves* (the qualities that meet the learning intention) and *amazings* (the qualities that would stretch students to go deeper). When teachers establish these clear success criteria, students are able to judge their performance and can see how their learning deepens when they go beyond expectation. Consider using examples and non-examples of student work to help clearly explain the success criteria.

Be mindful of students' academic identity. Students' past experiences with academic success and their perceived academic identity play a role in building self-efficacy. Listen for self-deprecating or negative self-reinforcing language, such as "I'm bad at math," "Everyone knows we're the dumb kids," and "I can't help that; I'm slow." Recognize that you will need to devote specific attention and time to those students to help reframe their thinking.

Make connections. Students may be unaware of how their success with one task can help them in other ways (e.g., how their success on a vocabulary assessment is useful for enhancing word choice in their next writing assignment). Help students see how their skills are related, so they can increase their self-efficacy across all aspects of learning.

Use language that builds students up. How the teacher speaks to students can either build up or tear down their feelings of self-efficacy. Consider these examples:

- Say this: "You are capable of doing anything you put your mind to. I've seen how determined you are."

- Not this: "You have a lot of potential, and I don't see you using it."

- Say this: "I see that your notebook is disorganized. Let's work together to put a different system in place so that you are prepared to learn every time you come to class."

- Not this: "Your notebook is a mess. It's no wonder you aren't ready to participate today."

QUICK START

	I can start this tomorrow!	I can begin this month	I need to discuss this with others	Resources needed
Integrate statements that build efficacy into instruction and feedback.				
Schedule regular intervals for students to self-assess their progress so they can see their academic growth.				
Include review and summarizing activities into every lesson to "empty their heads."				

CREATE CLASS AGREEMENTS

Teacher-generated class rules are developed by the teacher and then shared with the class. Many of us were taught in our own teacher preparation programs to have the rules listed for students from the very beginning. There's sound reasoning for having rules—and, importantly, using them consistently and fairly. A 2017 review of fifteen research articles on the characteristics of effective rules included these common practices:[10]

- Develop three to five positively stated rules and post them for all to see.

- Balance specificity with general rules that guide students. For instance, "Be respectful to each other" is general; "One voice at a time in discussion" is specific.

- Teach and reteach these throughout the year.

In the past decade or so, there has been an uptick among teachers in developing classroom agreements. These rules are reflective of agreed norms the class has mutually constructed with guidance from the teacher. They often include general norms, such as being respectful of others and the learning space, being prepared, and taking risks. You may even see student signatures at the bottom.

Like pretty much everything else in education, classroom agreements can be used poorly. They are not meant to be a *laisse-faire* style of classroom management, where the kids make all the decisions and anything goes. There's solid evidence that students want a wise, steady, compassionate adult in the room who is going to ensure the smooth operation of the classroom. You can start off the school year with your "non-negotiables" as a springboard for discussion of the classroom agreements. We start our year with three placeholders: *Take care of yourself. Take care of each other. Take care of this place.*

Two common types of class agreements are a class contract and a class motto. A class contract is a set of statements that everyone in the class agrees to live by; it clearly outlines the norms that are central to a community of learners. A class contract may include both agreed-on classroom expectations (the behavior and class environment everyone wants to uphold), as well as student responsibilities (what to do and how to support someone who isn't upholding the classroom expectations). The benefit of a class contract is that the teacher no longer is the sole person responsible for managing behavior. It now becomes the collective responsibility of the class to ensure that the expectations of the contract are being upheld.

Using the following procedures can help simplify the process. Initially, it may be helpful to write student ideas on sticky notes in order to sort and categorize them later. Begin by asking students to brainstorm expectations. These prompts can support idea generation:

- What kinds of actions will be most helpful for learning?
- How do you want others to treat you while you are at school?
- What kinds of actions will help everyone feel safe physically (our bodies) and emotionally (our feelings)?

Review the brainstormed list, and help students group similar ideas together. Discuss other ideas that may need to be consolidated, removed, or reworded. Once the list is pared down, work with students to generate sentences or statements that reflect the brainstormed ideas. Depending on the age of the students, sentence frames may be useful.

We appreciate the advice that Maine Teacher of the Year candidate Jeff Bailey offered in a blog on how he sparks reflective discussion among his high school students. He uses these questions, which allow further consideration from the group before they finalize their agreement:[11]

- Stand back and look. Are there any gaps?
- Are there any we cannot live with?
- Are there any here that are more important than others?

In addition to preparing a contract, it can be helpful to create a class motto. Students often recite a class motto daily at the start of the day or class period as a reminder of the agreed-on norms. This approach also serves as an opportunity for students to start fresh and on the right foot.

Develop the motto with students, and make sure it captures the spirit of the class agreement. Here are some effective class mottos we have seen over the years:

- We are different as individuals, and respect brings us together.
- Every fork in the road is a challenge and a choice.
- None of us is as great as all of us!
- Start where you are. Use what you have. Do what you can.
- We can do hard things.

Drawing on the research on self-affirmations,[12] repeating the motto out loud regularly can have positive effects on self-perception and motivation to uphold the values espoused in the motto.

Once agreements have been created, it is vital to reference and reinforce them often or they will cease to be significant. On a regular basis, you can make statements such as these:

- "I appreciate how _____ got organized for learning this morning. He/She/They are being mindful of our class agreement."

- "Let's notice that _____ is exemplifying one of our class agreement principles. He/She/They are showing respect toward _____ by _____."

Calling attention to these positive behaviors is also important because students who exhibit these behaviors may not even be aware of them. Not only is the teacher shining a light on an individual student and building them up, but also the teacher is encouraging other students to do the same.

TAKE ACTION

Examine your current class rules. Take a look at your current class rules and how they are written. Do they encourage compliance or ownership? Are they stated in positive ways rather than focusing on what students should not do?

Start simple. If creating a class contract seems like a huge shift for you, consider starting with a class motto. Have a discussion with students about what they believe represents the class.

Create sentence frames. Think about some sentence frames that might help you and your students write the motto or contract. For example, "In our class, we _____. We _____, _____, and _____. We _____ and _____. And most of all, we _____."

Don't wait! Although it is logical to create a class motto or class contract at the beginning of the school year or semester, they can be done at any point in the year. It is never too late to involve your students in this process.

QUICK START

	I can start this tomorrow!	I can begin this month	I need to discuss this with others	Resources needed
Read and discuss ways that colleagues have used class mottos, contracts, or agreements in their classes.				
Gather feedback from students about their learning and what agreements would better support them.				
Share classroom agreements, mottos, and contracts with families/caregivers.				

DEVELOP SUCCESS CRITERIA TO PROMOTE INVOLVEMENT

No matter what time of year it is that you find yourself reading this book, it's likely you have set some goals for yourself personally (e.g., drink more water, exercise regularly) or professionally (e.g., finish all grading at school, get a master's degree). Whatever you're aiming for, you will usually need to pair big goals with smaller incremental steps in order to be successful. This approach applies to the goals that our students set too.

Learning goals can definitely be motivating for students. Chase Nordengren, a research scientist at NWEA, notes that "while a teacher can never force students to apply themselves to the task of learning, there are many tools at the teacher's disposal to motivate and engage students in the hard work of learning. Goal setting brings these tools together into practice."[13]

However, when goals are too big or too far in the future, students have difficulty seeing progress.

As an example, "Getting an A in math this year" is too broad. Help students break statements like this down into smaller, more actionable steps that move them toward the larger goal. When students know where they need to go and how to get there, it becomes easier for them to assess their current level of understanding against the learning outcome.[14] These smaller, bite-sized chunks of learning goals are called *success criteria*, which give students a means to incrementally monitor their progress.

"I can" statements are one form of success criteria, and they have the added bonus that they contribute to cognitive restructuring through self-affirmations. Consider these incremental success criteria that move students forward through an elementary science unit on animal behavior:[15]

- *Success Criterion 1:* I can list different animal behaviors.

- *Success Criterion 2:* I can describe how animals gather food, find shelter, defend themselves, and rear their young.

- *Success Criterion 3:* I can use evidence to infer how these behaviors help animals to survive.

- *Success Criterion 4:* I can construct an explanation for why specific behaviors depend on specific habitats and environments.

It is useful to keep success criteria as specific and measurable as possible. This approach will make it easier for the teacher and students to monitor progress as well as to break down the goals into attainable steps. Students' motivation to accomplish their goals also increases when these four factors are considered:[16]

- **Competence:** Does the student believe that they can accomplish the goal?

- **Control/Autonomy:** Does the student have control over how they work to accomplish the goal?

- **Interest/Value:** Is the student interested in the goal or outcome, and do they see the value in attaining the goal?

- **Relatedness:** Does accomplishing the goal help the student feel a greater sense of belonging in the classroom or feel some other desired social benefit?

Ultimately, as students gain the ability to see where they were and where they are in relation to where they are going, they are more likely to take ownership of their learning[17] and their self-efficacy increases.[18]

TAKE ACTION

Use academic language that is developmentally appropriate. Success criteria can and should use the academic vocabulary students are learning. However, they shouldn't sound like standards. Standards are, first and foremost, much too big. Most standards take the better part of the school year to master. Further, standards are written for a different audience: other educators. Success criteria are written so that students understand them.

Provide methods for tracking and assessing their progress. Students will not see their progress unless they have some way to visualize it. This could be something as simple as a chart or checklist that they regularly complete, or students could use a notebook to record their progress. Another method is to have them compare their work to a rubric you have taught them or constructed with them. You can also gauge progress by asking learners to self-assess with exit slips.

QUICK START

	I can start this tomorrow!	I can begin this month	I need to discuss this with others	Resources needed
If you haven't done this before, learn from colleagues about how they use success criteria in their class.				
Read about success criteria in your content or grade level.				
Identify the instructional content you feel you are strongest in to experiment with success criteria.				

CASE IN POINT: CLASS MOTTO

It was late fall, and Ms. Lindholm was feeling frustrated that her students didn't seem to be taking the classroom rules to heart. She felt she was wasting a lot of instructional time reminding students of behavioral expectations. She shared her frustration with her assistant principal. During the discussion, the assistant principal suggested that involving her students in the creation of a class motto—the norms and expectations that everyone agrees to—might be a step toward increasing student ownership and involvement in their learning. Ms. Lindholm agreed this could be a good way to reset, and she and the assistant principal talked through how to implement that with her first graders.

The following Monday, Ms. Lindholm held a class meeting and explained that the class was going to create a motto that they would all agree to follow. She began by asking the class what kinds of behaviors were important for learning, and she recorded students' responses on a sheet of chart paper. She then asked students what kind of classroom environment they wanted to have to support their learning, and she recorded their responses on a separate sheet of chart paper.

On Tuesday, the class revisited their brainstormed ideas and worked together to group similar ideas, remove duplicates, and narrow things down to what they agreed were the most important elements. She then provided students with a paragraph frame that helped them form their motto:

In our class, we _____. We _____, _____, and _____.
We _____ and _____. And most of all, we _____.

Together, they decided on the following motto:

> *In our class, we love to learn. We work hard, do our best, and are not afraid to make mistakes. We are kind and respectful to each other. And most of all, we have fun!*

Ms. Lindholm was pleasantly surprised at how engaged and committed to the task her students were. She was even more pleased that students who didn't typically participate in group discussions were actively sharing ideas. Ms. Lindholm decided to have the class recite their motto together every morning, with the goal of memorizing it by the December winter break.

What's Your Advice?

- Ms. Lindholm has started using a class motto. What advice do you have for her to infuse it into instruction and feedback?

- What evidence do you suggest Ms. Lindholm watch for and listen for to signal that the class motto is having desired effects? How might she know if it needs to be revised?

- How might this look different in a secondary classroom?

WHAT'S NEXT?

ESSENTIAL QUESTION

How do we engage students actively with, and alongside, peers in shared learning and common goals?

THINK ABOUT

- How do we foster and maintain students' sense of self-efficacy in their learning?

- How can class agreements contribute to student ownership of learning and the classroom?

- How can success criteria be leveraged to involve students in their learning?

START – STOP – KEEP

Based on what you learned in this module, answer the questions that follow.

Start: What practice(s) would you like to start doing?
Stop: What practice(s) would you like to stop doing?
Keep: What practice(s) would you like to keep doing?

NOTES

9 HEARD

For students, being heard at school is not just about knowing that who they are speaking to is listening. Being heard is about knowing that who they are speaking to actually *wants* to hear what they have to say because the listener believes the student's voice is valuable. This listener is not just waiting for their next turn to talk. Instead, the listener demonstrates a fundamental belief that without the person's voice, opinion, and experience, the experience, learning, or sense of community is not complete. Students who feel heard know that they always have a seat at the table.

A trusting and open communication environment is key. Students must feel comfortable expressing their concerns without fear of being judged, graded negatively, or dismissed. If students have a bad experience sharing their voice, they will be less likely to share their thoughts in the future. Additionally, teachers must provide students with a wide variety of academic, social, and leadership experiences to help students clearly develop their understanding of their voice. The better students understand themselves, the better able they are to communicate effectively and confidently, and to advocate for themselves.[1]

In essence, students who feel heard know what they say matters and is valued. The more opportunities we create for students to feel heard, the more they feel a sense of belonging in their classroom, with their peers, and at their school. As their sense of belonging increases, they become more empowered to engage in classroom instruction, participate confidently in academic situations and school activities, take academic and social risks, and have consistent attendance at school.

HOW ARE WE SEEKING OUT ALL LEARNERS' PERSPECTIVES ON ISSUES THAT MATTER?

Indicators: Teachers described these indicators of a classroom and school environment where student voice is sought and acted on. Use these indicators to assess your own environment.

Table 9.1 • What Being Heard Looks, Sounds, and Feels Like

What Does It Look Like?	What Does It Sound Like?	What Does It Feel Like?
• Using interest surveys to inform curriculum • Seeking representation of voice • Leaning in • Using positive and accepting body language • Teachers supporting student-led conversations • Promoting autonomy through student jobs and roles in the classroom • Soliciting and acting on feedback from students • Engaging different perspectives • Student choice and decision-making in how they demonstrate understanding • Providing opportunities for open communication • Providing sentence frames for accountable talk	• Teachers being quiet (talking less) • Utilizing active listening skills • Being kindly persistent • Utilizing follow-up questions and prompting • Validating students' ideas, responses, and emotions • Asking students what they need • Using appropriate sentence frames/ language for accountable talk	• Understood • Valued • Considered • Respected • Purposeful • Productive • Powerful • Genuine

TWO TRUTHS AND A LIE

Two of these statements are true; one is false. Can you spot the lie?

1. Disengaged students attend school less, have lower self-concepts, achieve less academically, and are more likely to drop out of school.

2. One of the best ways for students to feel heard is to teach and use active listening skills, paying close attention to nonverbal communication.

3. Students possess unique knowledge and perspectives about their school and their educational experiences that adults cannot replicate without student partnership.

As adults and professionally trained educators, it is easy to assume that we know how to best meet our students' needs and support them in their academic and social-emotional development. While that may be true to a certain extent, students of all ages can provide us with valuable information about their interests, opinions, and personal experiences that we can access only if we ask them and truly listen and respect their responses.[2]

But without opportunity to be heard, students can feel anonymous in their schools and their classrooms and begin to believe that they are powerless to affect change or make decisions about their academic trajectory. These feelings of alienation and disengagement often lead to poor school attendance, low self-concept, and low academic achievement—and they can ultimately cause students to drop out of school entirely.[3]

Thus, the lie involves active listening.[4] Active listening strategies can help students feel their voice is being heard, but when teachers and peers use the strategies

(Continued)

(Continued)

without follow-through, students can still end up feeling judged or dismissed. Consider this four-step process instead:

1. **Actively Listen:** Use effective listening strategies, such as eye contact, head nodding, open body posture, and affirming nonverbal communication cues.

2. **Validate:** When a student shares thoughts, opinions, or concerns, validate them. This doesn't mean you have to agree, but it is important they know you value their voice.

3. **Connect:** When possible, make a personal or general connection to what the student shares. Most people feel good when others can make connections to something they said.

4. **Transition:** Be careful not to transition away from the topic too soon. Doing so can make the student feel dismissed. Instead, skillfully bridge their thoughts to another topic.

Here are two different responses a sixth-grade teacher might make to a student who asks, "Why can't lunchtime be two hours long?" Think about which response encourages student voice and which dismisses feedback and questioning.

Sample A: "Two hours? That will never happen. We already extended lunch by five minutes two years ago. Even if you're the last person in line and you're a slow eater, you can easily finish before the bell rings. I promise you. Hey, I have to run. I'll see you in fifth period."

Sample B: "I imagine many students would enjoy a longer lunchtime. No one likes to feel rushed to eat or stop socializing with close friends. I certainly don't. Because schools are required to provide a specific number of instructional minutes, the cost of extending lunch would be setting our alarm clocks earlier and staying at school longer in the afternoon. Does that make sense? [Pause for a response.] Speaking of lunch, how do you like the new pizza? I've heard good things about it from other students, but I haven't tried it yet. Do you recommend it?"

RESTORATIVE CIRCLES

Imagine these three scenarios:

- a group of people at a social function having a casual conversation;

- colleagues in a boardroom who are problem solving a corporate challenge; and

- passersby gathering around a street performer.

Chances are that all these groups formed some sort of circle. Circles provide an opportunity for everyone to be seen and to see others without an obstructed view. They also allow for conversation to organically flow more easily because body language and nonverbal cues can be viewed by everyone.

The concept of a restorative circle is derived from indigenous cultures across the world.[5] The purpose is to provide everyone in the circle the opportunity to speak and share their thoughts related to a specific topic. Rather than one person having the power to drive the discussion, in the circle everyone is considered equal, and all information shared is valuable. In our classrooms, circles provide the opportunity for everyone to be heard—not just the same five students who always like to speak.

One key element of the restorative circle is the use of a talking piece. It provides structure for the circle and signals who will talk next during the discussion. Anyone without the talking piece must listen respectfully and attentively to the speaker to allow the speaker's thoughts to be fully heard and recognized.

To try this approach, use a talking piece that is an object of significance to your class. For example, it could be a bookmark to signal the shared value of reading, or it might be a harmonica because you often listen to music together in class. The talking piece can even change periodically throughout the year as you and your class grow together.

There are three main types of restorative circles:[6]

- **Sequential Circles:** The entire class creates one large circle in the room. After the teacher shares the prompt or discussion question, they give one student the talking piece. That student shares what they would like to say and then passes the talking piece to the person next to them, until all students around the circle have shared. A student may pass the talking piece without sharing, but typically all students respond. If some students passed during discussion, the talking piece may be given back to them later to contribute.

- **Nonsequential Circles:** The entire class creates one large circle in the room. After the teacher provides the prompt or discussion question, one student begins with the talking piece and shares what they would like to say. The talking piece moves anywhere around the circle, as students volunteer to share.

- **Inside Outside Circles:** The class is divided into two equal groups. The students make two circles, one inside the other, and the two circles face each other. After the prompt or discussion question is shared, each pair of students facing each other discusses it. When discussion is finished, the outside circle stays still, and the inside circle moves one person to the right, providing each student with a new discussion partner. The rotation continues as appropriate to the topic being discussed or as the lesson requires.

Circles can function in two ways: reactive and proactive. In a reactive approach, students are sharing their voice in response to a social situation that needs to be discussed (e.g., cliques during recess or a hate crime in the community) or are reacting to instruction (e.g., responding to questions about a text that was read or discussing understanding of a topic being studied). In a proactive approach, a circle is used to allow for student voices to be heard in order to reach consensus about decisions that affect them. For example, a circle may be used at the beginning of the year or semester to gain student input on class agreements, or to discuss an academic topic of study.

TAKE ACTION

Be strategic in how you pose questions. It is important to craft questions that students can respond deeply to and that avoid one-word responses. Open-ended questions are more inviting and allow students to think more deeply about the situations being discussed in a circle.

Have a wide range of questions prepared. You may find that a question falls flat or you don't get the type of responses you were anticipating. Prepare several questions in advance to ensure that the conversation moves forward and stays fresh.

Use the strategy often. Don't save restorative circles for when there is a problem. Use them proactively, such as to discuss learning on yesterday's field trip or to discuss an upcoming event. The more students engage in circles, the more comfortable they will be with the structure and their willingness to share.

Take note of students who pass. It is always okay for a student to pass the talking stick. However, if you notice a pattern with individual students, consider encouraging them ahead of time. Use language such as, "Hey, we are going to be doing a circle about _____ tomorrow. Your voice is really important to the conversation, and I would love for you to consider sharing when it's your turn."

Use restorative circles outside of the classroom. Circles can be used with other groups of students outside of the classroom, such as with the afterschool clubs and sports teams.

QUICK START

	I can start this tomorrow!	I can begin this month	I need to discuss this with others	Resources needed
Schedule circles for academic and social-emotional purposes at least biweekly.				
Identify themes for each of the circles.				
Gather questions that will help to propel discussions.				

DEVELOPING STUDENT VOICE AND AGENCY

Student voice is defined as students' genuine input in their education. This pertains to instructional topics and opportunities and methods for learning. Importantly, it requires that students are involved in leadership roles to make decisions about policies and systems that can result in meaningful change in a school.[7]

Each student possesses unique knowledge and perspectives, including what impacts their learning, engagement, and mental wellness. They also bring unique identities, experiences, and strengths. When a school adopts practices that integrate student voice throughout its various systems, students have the opportunity to make a real impact on consequential issues that concern them. This is especially important for students who have been historically marginalized.[8] Student agency—the ability to choose and make self-determined decisions—is closely related to student voice. Agency increases as students begin to know that their thoughts, feelings, and ideas are important and that their actions have a direct effect on the outcomes.

For student voice to be fully realized, we must be intentional about creating opportunities to seek out the diverse voices of all students, not just a select few. With time, students will believe that their input from instructional topics to policies and practices are an important component to the overall success of the school and classroom. We are not suggesting that students take on the role of a school administrator, but there is tremendous value when student voice becomes an intentional component of key decisions related to learning, engagement, mental wellness, and other policy decisions that directly affect learners.

Safety and trust are two essential elements that affect students' willingness to speak honestly and to believe that their voice actually matters.[9] Although a student may feel safe to speak to a particular teacher, they may not feel heard when it comes to other factors that impact their experiences in school (e.g., social challenges, extracurricular activities, or school policies). Safety and trust can be fostered through low-stakes opportunities for students to share feedback and ideas. This may also be done confidentially to give students who tend to be shy—or who are still unsure whether their voice will be valued without judgment—an opportunity to respond.

Another way to build student voice is through the use of surveys that contain questions directly tied to a specific concept or topic. Depending on their use, surveys may be created by teachers, by students, or in collaboration. At the classroom level, surveys can examine ideas related to instruction (e.g., understanding of a unit of instruction) or to classroom climate (e.g., the use of instructional techniques such as small-group discussions or how often music is played during the day).

At the school level, surveys can be administered to the entire student body or to a specific group of students. One example is a school climate survey, which is used to monitor how students are feeling and to identify larger trends that may hinder learning, engagement, and wellness. Many states and districts require annual school climate surveys so that schools can monitor conditions. But conducting a classroom or school climate survey in and of itself is not the action that helps students feel heard. Imagine a student who indicated on a climate survey that they feel unsafe due to bullying related to their ethnicity and family/caregiver structure, only to continue experiencing the same treatment the following year. When the student does not witness direct actions by school staff that result in improved feelings of safety, the tool loses its power.

The quantitative results that any survey provides are incredibly helpful—but only if the results are adequately analyzed and acted on to improve outcomes for students. That means that students believe the information gathered by surveys will be used in ways that benefit them. Further, make sure that students know that their insights influenced decisions and actions.

TAKE ACTION

Ask for feedback and make a plan to implement it. Whether you create a formal survey or use a quick exit ticket, carefully consider how you will use the information you collect. It is also important to share with students how you are using their feedback.

Take note of students you haven't connected with yet and seek them out. If you notice students who continually hold back from sharing feedback or participating in discussions, make time to meet with them one-on-one. Ask questions to learn more about why they are holding back, encourage participation, and seek ways to build trust and safety.

Remind students their voice matters. Seek authentic opportunities to bring up students' past contributions to learning. Make statements such as "Do you remember when _____ said _____?" or "Yesterday, _____ made an important comment about _____. Let's think about that again as we discuss _____ today."

Provide structured and open opportunities for students to share their thoughts. Consider having a suggestion box where students can provide feedback. This allows students to share their thoughts freely, and it gives you an opportunity to carefully consider how to best attend to their feedback. Or have a weekly open reflection, such as a *celebration* (something that the student feels went well), a *challenge* (something the student wishes had gone differently), and a *let it go* (something else the student wants to share).

QUICK START

	I can start this tomorrow!	I can begin this month	I need to discuss this with others	Resources needed
Identify a classroom matter you would like feedback about, and design a survey or an exit ticket to gain students' thoughts.				
Share results of the feedback and discuss it with the class.				
Implement the suggestion and make sure students see the results.				

STUDENT EMPOWERMENT AND LEADERSHIP

Student voice is a powerful lever for learning and for school improvement. Yet it is uncommon for students to be involved in decision-making at their school. Student empowerment provides students with opportunities to influence decisions that will shape their academic lives at school and in the community. Unfortunately, student leadership and student government are often "misconceptualized as merely a pedagogical exercise revolving around simulated political arenas with little to no immediate real political consequence."[10] The emphasis is on simulating parliamentary procedures, rather than on decision-making about things that matter. Philosophically, there is a crucial distinction between structures designed to "develop future leaders" and those that recognize students for the leaders they are right now.

There are usually a handful of students whom the adults in the school would describe as "student leaders." The majority remain passive consumers of schooling, passing through the halls with a minimal investment in the organization. And who could blame them? We rarely ask students to get involved with anything of lasting consequence. The result is that adults work really hard trying to effect positive change but overlook their primary customers: the students themselves.

Youth empowerment researcher Adam Fletcher asks us to consider these indicators of meaningful involvement among students in their school:[11]

- Students are allies and partners with adults in improving schools.
- Students have the training and authority to create real solutions to the challenges that schools face in learning, teaching, and leadership.

- Schools, including educators and administrators, are accountable to the direct consumers of schools: students themselves.

- Student–adult partnerships are a major component of every sustainable, responsive, and systemic approach to transforming schools.

Opportunities abound at every level of schooling, including those we have listed in the following chart.

Table 9.2 • Opportunities for Students to Be Heard at Every Level of Schooling

Elementary Schools
• Membership in the school improvement committee
• Co-constructed curricular units reflecting student interests
• Student-led family/caregiver conferences
• Student classroom governance (e.g., class meetings)
• Student jobs in the front office, in the library, on the safety patrol, or as school ambassadors
• Student-led signature campaigns on civic engagement issues

Middle Schools
• Membership in all school committees
• Co-teaching
• Co-design and implementation of whole-school forums
• Service learning for the school community
• Agenda items for a school improvement committee submitted by students

High Schools
• Student representation on district committees, including budget committees
• Co-planning on course design
• Participation in professional development
• Membership in professional learning communities
• Positions on teacher and school leader hiring teams
• Design and implementation of whole-school forums about school and community issues
• Student-led educational conferences

TAKE ACTION

Gauge the status of student empowerment in your classroom and at your school. Begin by cataloging the ways students are currently involved in classroom, school, and community matters. You may discover that there are higher levels of community empowerment after school than during the school day.

Once current opportunities have been identified, evaluate the experience for students. What is the degree of meaningful student involvement? Use the quality indicators developed by Adam Fletcher in the chart as a yardstick for a self-study.

Empower students at the classroom level. Make students part of decisions in their classroom. Young children can help you make decisions about the classroom setup, such as what should be in the quiet corner and how the classroom should be decorated. Hold class meetings regularly to learn about students' concerns in their community and what actions they might take as a group. Embed civics and civic engagement into the curriculum, such as discussing fair voting procedures during class meetings or how classroom problems are resolved (e.g., cutting in line, leaving supplies disorganized so that the next period has to do the cleaning up).

QUICK START

	I can start this tomorrow!	I can begin this month	I need to discuss this with others	Resources needed
Develop student jobs that require decision-making and leadership, not just labor.				
Have students lead discussions in circles, Socratic seminar, or other formal discussion protocols you use.				
Set up classroom student committees (e.g., school spirit committee, recycling committee, social media committee).				

CASE IN POINT: STUDENT DRESS CODE

The focus of last month's staff meeting at River High School was results from the recent school climate data gathered from students during the mid-year point. The data showed that student responses related to their feelings of school connectedness decreased by 21 percent compared to the beginning of the year.

Following the meeting, the ninth-grade English department decided to tailor their upcoming persuasive essay assignment to activate student recommendations on improving their sense of belonging. While grading the assignment, it became clear to the team that several practices and policies contributed to the troubling survey data. They also agreed that many students had compelling recommendations for the school.

For example, several students focused their essays on how the current school dress code policy had negatively impacted students based on student identities and ethnic hairstyles, particularly among Black

and African American girls. Some students also claimed that language in the policy reinforced high rates of sexual harassment that many students experienced on campus based on their clothing choice. One student said it best: "School dress codes should not reinforce gender stereotypes or increase the marginalization or oppression of any group based on race, ethnicity, religion, gender identity, sexual orientation, household income or cultural observance. Our student body is diverse, and the policy should respect that." Another student included the results of an informal survey she administered during lunchtime with the following results:

1. Have you felt harmed by the current dress code policy?
   a. Yes: 72%
   b. No: 16%
   c. Not sure: 12%

2. Would you support a new dress code policy that is gender-neutral and that removes language to prevent biased discipline based on race, ethnicity, religion, gender and gender expression, and sexual orientation?
   a. Yes: 88%
   b. No: 7%
   c. Not sure: 5%

What's Your Advice

- What recommendations would you make to the ninth-grade English teachers based on what students shared in their persuasive essays?

- How can the teachers continue to respect student voice by including them in these next steps?

WHAT'S NEXT?

ESSENTIAL QUESTION

How are we seeking out all learners' perspectives on issues that matter?

THINK ABOUT

- In what ways can circles be used to support student voice both academically and socially?

- In what ways is student voice sought out at your school? What actions resulted because of student voice?

- What opportunities for student leadership exist beyond formal student governance structures such as Student Council?

START – STOP – KEEP

Based on what you learned in this module, answer the questions that follow.

Start: What practice(s) would you like to start doing?
Stop: What practice(s) would you like to stop doing?
Keep: What practice(s) would you like to keep doing?

NOTES

NEEDED

The desire to feel needed is a prosocial behavior marked by an intention to benefit others. However, prosocial behaviors move in two directions. Young children look for reciprocity as they learn to give and receive help from their others. Sharing is an early prosocial behavior that leads to more altruistic gestures. A sense of altruism is the desire to help others even when there is no direct benefit to self. Our society functions in part because we reciprocate, and in part because we are altruistic.

The absence of opportunities to reciprocate can be destructive. When someone is routinely on the receiving end of help, but routinely not able to reciprocate, the imbalance can provoke feelings of guilt and even anger. Consider the interactions you've had with toddlers. They want to help, whether it is sorting the laundry or making breakfast. There's an innate need to be helpful. Concepts such as sharing materials and cooperating with others to achieve tasks are fundamental for classroom productivity and learning.

The desire to help others is fueled by a sense of empathy or the ability to accurately understand what another person is feeling. It is "feeling with another."[1] Teachers foster empathy in several ways, such as taking care of a classroom pet, pointing out the victim's perspective when a conflict takes place, and choosing literature that provides students with opportunities to take on the perspectives of different characters.

Heightened empathy for others is, not surprisingly, associated with lower levels of aggressive behavior toward peers, including a higher likelihood that they will intervene in a bullying situation they witness.[2] But students need lots of ways to make their empathy actionable. In other words, our students need classroom structures that allow them to give and receive help.

Essential Question:

HOW ARE WE RECOGNIZING AND RECEIVING ALL OUR LEARNERS' TALENTS, GIFTS, AND CONTRIBUTIONS?

Indicators: Teachers described these indicators of a classroom and school environment where students feel needed. Use these indicators to assess your own environment.

Table 10.1 • What Being Needed Looks, Sounds, and Feels Like

What Does It Look Like?	What Does It Sound Like?	What Does It Feel Like?
• Helping a teacher or peer • Collaborating on assignments and tasks • Specifically acknowledging and recognizing active participation • Recognizing student strengths regularly • Utilizing peer tutoring • Utilizing roles and responsibilities for collective classroom success	• Acknowledging others' strengths • Using helping language (asking for help, offering help, accepting help, declining help) • Peer-to-peer conversations	• Important • Validated • Empty when someone's not there • Indispensable • Included

TWO TRUTHS AND A LIE

Two of these statements are true; one is false. Can you spot the lie?

1. Feeling needed by, and useful to, family/caregivers and friends does not differ across demographic groups, is associated with greater received support, and predicts psychological well-being above and beyond received support.

2. Peer assistance is associated with higher levels of motivation among students who are lower achieving.

3. Mentoring is useful for the mentee but does not extend to other aspects of the person's life.

In his book *The Educated Mind*, educational theorist Kieran Egan argued that development from childhood to young adulthood is driven by the learner's need to answer these three questions:[3]

- *Who am I?* Learners seek to answer questions about themselves. Consequently, they are fascinated with the functions of the body and with themselves in general. Hence, we see lots of "All About Me" curricula in the earliest grades.

- *How big is the world?* Children take the measure of the world, asking *How big? How long? How small? How wide?* They are eager to soak up all the curious/amazing/gross facts about the world.

- *What is my place in the world?* The third major pursuit combines the knowledge they are gaining and ultimately seeks to answer this question: *Where do I fit?* As students learn about themselves and of the span of the world, each strives to find the niche that fits them best.

The third question is also at the heart of feeling needed, and there is solid research to back it up. Adolescents who report feeling needed by family/caregivers and friends have a greater sense of well-being that goes beyond the amount of support they receive. When young people are able to provide support back to others and not just receive it, this interaction makes a difference "at a time of life when they are seeking to establish their place in the social world."[4]

Peer assistance and peer-tutoring classroom systems enhance opportunities to help and are seen by other students as a motivation for learning, especially among those who are not yet at expected levels.[5] Why? They know they are not alone in their learning endeavors.

And as we have noted before, the benefits of peer tutoring go a long way. The lie, then, is the third statement. Elementary and middle school children who are being mentored by an older student or by an adult score higher on measures of empathy, generosity, cognitive functioning, and prosocial behavior than those who do not have a mentor.[6] Helping, receiving help, and mentoring, we argue, can help young people answer the three questions Egan proposed.

THE HELPING CURRICULUM

There's much discussion among educators and employers about the social and emotional skills needed for learning, employment, and life. Often called *soft skills*, these include empathy, collaboration, ethics, communication, and self-management.[7] However, it can be difficult for educators to teach these soft skills directly, at least compared to teaching multiplication or how to infer an author's meaning in a text. One challenge is that being able to *identify* soft skills isn't enough. Students must be able to put those skills into action on a regular basis. And students, especially younger ones, need ways to take these abstract ideas and make them concrete. Enter the helping curriculum.[8]

The helping curriculum was originally conceived as a way to assist teachers in developing inclusive practices that preserve the dignity and rights of children with disabilities in general education classrooms. The underlying principle is that all people, regardless of age or ability, need to know how to ask for help, offer help, accept help, and politely decline help.

We have used the helping curriculum successfully with primary students as well as those in high school. We introduce these principles to our students and provide developmentally appropriate examples and non-examples of each. Students also enjoy offering their own examples of each, and we find it is a good way to learn more about one another. Posters like the following serve as reminders of what is required whenever students work with others.

Here are some language stems our students have suggested for each of the helping categories.[9]

Ways to Ask for Help

- I'm stuck. Can you help me get unstuck?
- I tried this but it isn't working so far. Do you have an idea?
- I don't understand this. Do you?

Ways to Offer Help

- Can I help?
- I have an idea. Would you like to hear it?
- I can help with that, if you want.

Ways to Accept Help

- Thank you.
- I appreciate your help.
- I am glad you came along!

Ways to Decline Help

- Thank you. I think I have it.
- Thank you. I want to try just a little bit longer.
- Thank you. I need a few more minutes. If I still don't get it, can we talk again?

TAKE ACTION

Teach the helping curriculum proactively and use these practices every day. You know best how these routines should be expressed in your classroom. Too often, they are left unstated until a problem arises. Proactively teaching your helping routines can head off tears, defensiveness, and misunderstandings.

Ask your students what they need. Your students are a great source of information and insight. If they are old enough, teach them what soft skills are, and ask students for advice about how the soft skills can be enhanced in their classroom. For younger students, talk about how teams work together to be successful.

Make the helping curriculum part of weekly exit tickets. Use exit tickets weekly to pose questions to students about the helping curriculum. Ask them to describe a time in the previous five days when they asked for help, offered help, accepted help, or politely declined help. Track responses and meet with individual students who rarely have examples so you can learn how to better support them in their efforts.

QUICK START

	I can start this tomorrow!	I can begin this month	I need to discuss this with others	Resources needed
Discuss what helping means (e.g., "How can you help someone without telling them the answer?") and what it means to receive help.				
Survey your class to identify authentic times when a helping curriculum can occur.				
Schedule time weekly (e.g., exit ticket, class meeting) to discuss when students had opportunities to do each of the four helping dimensions.				

PEER TUTORING

One of the ways to ensure that students feel needed is to let them experience the thrill of tutoring a peer. Many years ago, Doug was assigned a group of students for a class called "remedial reading." All students enrolled in this class were reading three or more years below the expected grade. The students who were required to take this class did not take an elective, such as music or art. Educators have long known that segregating students in this way is counterproductive, yet the school leadership was desperate to improve reading performance and wanted to try. Thus, "remedial programs [such as the one Doug was teaching] can function to preserve the status quo by protecting the structures of schooling—and, by implication, the society in which schools reside—from social criticism."[10] That does not mean that no students need intervention, but there are more effective intervention models.[11]

Long story short, Doug turned the class into a peer-tutoring experience and partnered with a local elementary school where the students in his class could teach reading to students in kindergarten and first grade. The older learners wrote books to share with the younger students, and they improved their own reading in the process. However, what was most powerful was the adolescents' reflection on being needed. Each student noted this was the first time that they experienced the thrill of teaching. They had been the receivers of help for years, and this experience taught them that they had things to offer others. As one of them said, "I didn't think anybody really needed me. At least at school. Like what do I have? But they did. And I helped. Like, really, I got them to know the letters and words." As the French essayist Joseph Joubert purportedly said, "To teach is to learn twice."

Overall, peer tutoring has a positive impact on learning. There is an effect size of 0.54 on the person receiving the tutoring and an effect size of 0.48 on the person doing the tutoring. And peer tutoring is free! What a bargain—to get that much value from something that doesn't cost money yet increases students' understanding that they are needed and that they belong.

Of course, there are other models of peer tutoring besides cross-age systems. Here are a few examples:

- **Class Wide Peer Tutoring (CWPT):** At specific times each week, the class is divided into groups of two to five students. The goal is to practice or review skills and content, rather than to introduce new learning. Each student in the group has an opportunity to be both the tutee and the tutor.[12]

- **Peer Assisted Learning Strategies (PALS):** Pairs of students work together, taking turns tutoring and being tutored. Teachers train students to use the following learning strategies for reading: passage reading with partners, paragraph "shrinking" (or describing the main idea), and prediction relay (predicting what is likely to happen next in the passage).[13]

- **Reciprocal Peer Tutoring (RPT):** Students are paired at random to support the learning of their peers. It's essentially a collaborative learning task that involves students with similar academic backgrounds working together. Each partnership is responsible for synthesizing content; preparing tasks; and asking questions, complete with answers and explanation. Often students develop practice tests during RPT and then identify areas of additional learning needed.[14]

TAKE ACTION

The following points are useful as you plan and implement a peer-tutoring program in your classroom:[15]

- *Clarify the specific objectives of the tutoring program,* including both academic and social objectives when appropriate.

- *List objectives in a form that can be easily measured.* Here are two examples.

  ○ "Students serving as tutees will improve reading fluency by 30 percent on classroom reading materials in the next twelve weeks."

  ○ "Performance of all students on weekly spelling tests will improve to an average of 85 percent; no student will score lower than 60 percent."

- **Choose tutoring partners carefully.** No firm conclusions can be drawn to direct tutoring choices. Some teachers have recommended choosing students as tutors who are conscientious in class, and who generally have to work for their grades. Other considerations include the compatibility of the tutoring pair. Teachers should find pairs who will work together well. Pairing students who are different in gender, race, or socioeconomic status whenever possible helps build social cohesion in the classroom.

- **Establish rules and procedures for the tutoring program.** These rules should cover how students are to interact with each other, and they should specify the type of interactions that are not acceptable. Procedures should specify the times and dates of tutoring, the materials to be used, and the specific activities to be undertaken.

- **Implement the tutoring program, monitor it carefully, and be consistent in enforcing the rules and procedures.** Modify rules and procedures as necessary.

- **Evaluate the program frequently,** and do not wait for the end of the program to determine whether it was effective. Collect information throughout the program and predict whether it will be successful. If progress is not being made, modify the program.

QUICK START

	I can start this tomorrow!	I can begin this month	I need to discuss this with others	Resources needed
Decide what peer-tutoring model would work best in your class.				
Train tutors and tutees.				
Schedule time weekly to devote to peer tutoring.				

CROSS-AGE MENTORING

The practice of mentoring, which is pairing an older and more experienced person with a younger novice, has endured throughout human history. Trades and professions continue to use this to onboard and support newer employees as they learn their craft. Many youth organizations provide similar mentoring programs for children and adolescents outside of school, such as scouting, Boys and Girls Clubs, as well as those locally sponsored by community and religious organizations.

But mentorship of students by students during the school day is a relatively newer phenomenon. These cross-age mentoring programs pair older students (at least two years older) with younger ones in the school to provide extra guidance, support, and a chance to give as well as receive. Students selected to receive the support of mentors may be at higher risk for not feeling a sense of belonging in schools.

There are successful examples of cross-age mentoring programs across the country that specialize in children of incarcerated parents, Native American and Alaska Native youth, and immigrant and refugee youth, to name just a few.[16] There are several advantages to these programs, and some are practical, such as the low cost. Other key benefits to mentors and mentees include the following.[17,18,19]

Table 10.2 • Benefits for Mentors and Mentees

Benefits for Mentors	Benefits for Mentees
Increased sense of belonging in school	Increased sense of belonging in school
Growth in feeling needed	Increased academic competence
Growth in empathy	Improved grades and attendance
Better communication and conflict resolution skills	Improved prosocial behaviors, especially empathy and proving help
Strengthened relationships with family/caregivers	

Cross-aged mentoring programs differ from cross-aged tutoring in that these programs are not strictly academic. Rather, the focus is on relational trust. These mentoring programs may be organized around an activity, such as music or gaming. Students selected to be mentored are often those who struggle academically and/or behaviorally. Students selected to be mentors do not need to be academically at the top of their class or to hold formal student leadership roles. However, they should possess qualities that would provide a positive experience for the mentee.

Because cross-age mentoring programs typically occur weekly or twice a month for the entire school year, the potential mentor's availability should also be considered. The National Mentoring Resource Center advises that potential mentors should apply for the position and be interviewed to determine their dispositions, interest, and commitment.[20] Successful cross-age mentoring programs provide mentors with training and adult support and supervision. In many schools, students who serve as mentors earn service credit on their transcript. Mentees should also be recruited, and this step begins with identifying who your target group should be. These may be students who are facing personal or academic challenges.

TAKE ACTION

Find a partner at your school who is interested in cross-aged mentoring.
If you teach students in the lower grades at your school, find an upper-grade teacher. If the circumstances are reversed, locate a colleague in a younger grade level.

Identify resources you can use. The Nation Mentoring Resource Center, sponsored by the US Department of Education, has great resources for designing and implementing a cross-age mentoring program at your school. They offer training and technical assistance, as well as useful materials for training mentors, designing activities for them to use, and monitoring program success.[21,22]

QUICK START

	I can start this tomorrow!	I can begin this month	I need to discuss this with others	Resources needed
Hold discussions with colleagues from other grade levels about their interest in cross-age mentoring.				
Examine resources for mentoring curricula at https://nationalmentoring resourcecenter.org/ resources-for-mentoring-programs/.				
Discuss cross-age mentoring with your school's administrator, school counselor, or social worker and with the Parent-Teacher Organization to enlist support, ideas, and resources.				

CASE IN POINT: CROSS-AGE MENTORING AT CASEY ELEMENTARY SCHOOL

The staff at Casey Elementary, a TK–6 school, were interested in building belonging across the school. Several of them attended a summer conference and struck up a conversation with members from Lincoln Elementary, a school in another state. Their new colleagues told them about a cross-age mentoring program they had been implementing for several years, including the successes they had experienced and challenges they had faced. When the Casey Elementary staff returned to school for the new academic year, they formed a working committee on cross-age mentoring. They scheduled a virtual meeting with members of the Lincoln mentoring group and, in preparation,

decided to prepare questions for the discussion with their more experienced colleagues.

What's Your Advice?

Help them by advising on some questions they should ask about the following:

- Recruitment, screening, and selection of mentors

- Supervision of the program

- Training mentors

- Quality indicators

- Family/Caregiver communication

WHAT'S NEXT?

ESSENTIAL QUESTION

How are we recognizing and receiving all our learners' talents, gifts, and contributions?

THINK ABOUT

- How could you implement a helping curriculum in your classroom?
- What potential academic needs could a peer-tutoring program address in your grade level?
- Which students in your school could benefit from a cross-age peer mentoring program (mentors and mentees)?

START – STOP – KEEP

Based on what you learned in this module, answer the questions that follow.

Start: What practice(s) would you like to start doing?

Stop: What practice(s) would you like to stop doing?

Keep: What practice(s) would you like to keep doing?

NOTES

now that i know you exist,
how do i not love you
- butterflies rising, *wild spirit, soft heart*

LOVED

The English language, for all its virtues, lacks the nuance needed to cover the expanse of the word *love*. A single word is meant to signify a complicated concept, so we glue on other words to better describe what we really mean: *love of family*, *love of country*, *romantic love*, and so on. The ancient Greek language had distinctly different words to describe dimensions of love: *Xenia* signified the ethical responsibility of hospitality extended to travelers, while *philia* was used to describe friendships between equals (think *affiliation*). Then there is *eros*, which is the intimacy between romantic partners.

Love in the context of education is more closely aligned with *storge* and *agape*. The word *storge* describes the kind of parental love that all children need to experience in order to thrive. In fact, schooling is deeply rooted in the legal concept of in loco parentis ("in place of the parent"), which requires educators to take over some of the functions of a parent/caregiver by acting in the best interests of a child in their care. *Agape* is the highest form of love and describes the charity and affection shown for all humans. As educators we strive to accomplish both *storge* and *agape* as part of our ethics of our profession. Educational philosopher Nel Noddings, a major contributor to the theory of the ethics of care in education, wrote,

> Good schools, like good parents, should give far more attention to the social and moral development of students and, in general, to the sort of society they are promoting—one that will help citizens to develop and retain an intact morality.[1]

At its heart, education is infused with these concepts of love and ethics. To love our students is to hold them with unconditional positive regard, to foster trust with them and their community, and to engage in a collective responsibility to all, not just those currently on our roster. In doing so, we ensure that belonging is a perpetual investment, today and every day.

Indicators: Teachers described these indicators of a classroom and school environment where every child is loved for who they are. Use these indicators to assess your own environment.

Table 11.1 • What Being Loved Looks, Sounds, and Feels Like

What Does It Look Like?	What Does It Sound Like?	What Does It Feel Like?
• Utilizing supportive physical or verbal acknowledgment	• Sharing words of affirmation	• Warm and fuzzy
• Showing patience, effort, and unity	○ "I care for you"	• Like home
• Demonstrating empathy and compassion	○ "I hear you"	• Safe, yet vulnerable
• Providing comfort	• Sharing words of validation	• Encouraged
• Building meaningful relationships	○ "You're allowed to feel . . ."	• Authentic
• Sharing warm greetings and interactions	• Sharing affective statements	• Unconditional
• Giving students grace and forgiveness before anything else	○ "I feel . . ."	
	• Making statements of empathy	
	• Giving words of grace and forgiveness	

TWO TRUTHS AND A LIE

Two of these statements are true; one is false. Can you spot the lie?

1. Students have a lot of exposure to ways people build peaceful societies.

2. Adult modeling is an essential process for young children to learn and develop their own character strengths.

3. Teacher immediacy is associated with student motivation to learn.

Sadly, you probably spotted the lie right away. It's the first statement. One analysis of US history textbooks found that eighty-nine of one hundred pages were devoted to war topics; only five pages were on peace and peacemakers.[2] Although conflict topics are important, we must also ensure that students learn about how conflict can be repaired and avoided. If schools are to be reflective of a society we strive to be, then students need to see how caring is exhibited in their everyday experiences.

Fortunately, teachers are able models of how love and caring are enacted.[3] From a developmental standpoint, the ways adults model these actions can have a profound positive effect on students. A caring climate, which is to say one in which every student and every adult feels they belong, is grounded in a belief that prioritizes human needs.

In classrooms, educators can address these needs by creating a solid sense of trust and immediacy. To create a sense of trust, teachers must demonstrate relatability, honesty, and the mindset of holding the students' best interests at heart. To demonstrate immediacy—our approachability and the way we are close and responsive—we can make sure our behaviors include eye contact, friendly facial expressions, supportive gestures, near proximity to students, and a warm speaking tone. Many of these immediacy behaviors are nonverbal, but they are instantly detectable by students, because the actions convey the respect, love, and high regard we hold for students. In classrooms where the teacher maintains consistent immediacy, students are more motivated to learn.[4]

The concept of unconditional positive regard, which recognizes that humans are fallible and that we are loved despite our fallibility, was developed by psychologist Carl Rogers as a foundational underpinning of person-centered counseling.[5] In any guiding relationship—be it counselor and patient, parent/caregiver and child, or teacher and student—unconditional positive regard is a universal human need. By exhibiting unconditional positive regard, we allow ourselves to act with empathy—which Rogers stated is the key to having a positive impact on another. The message is simple even though its execution is not: *empathy leads to change*.

Unconditional regard should not be confused with unconditional acceptance. A student who plagiarizes an English essay or the child who is casually cruel to a classmate has acted in a way that is not acceptable. But unconditional regard separates the actor from the action to create a way forward for the young person. Students may have consequences for their actions, but teachers who practice unconditional regard pair these steps with the compassionate discussion of why it might have happened and how productive alternatives could be used in the future. Through this approach, students can redeem themselves and learn.

The use of unconditional positive regard is not confined to conflict and problematic behavior. While classroom teachers are not trained counselors, this principle permeates educational theory. You use it each time you provide growth-producing feedback. When a student makes an error on a math problem, you respond by saying, "You're nearly there, but there's a step that's getting in the way. Let's go back and think together about what you already know about this problem. You're going to solve this in no time!" The warmth and optimism you display to that young mathematician, along with your content knowledge, gives them confidence to try again. And if you're seeing the roots of unconditional positive regard in growth mindset, you're correct.

Unconditional positive regard is essential for a thriving learner-centered classroom, described as a "perspective that couples a focus on individual learners . . . with a focus on learning."[6] A learner-centered classroom is led by a teacher who views students warmly, and with dignity. Learner-centered classrooms are associated with many of the things we care most about in education, including higher achievement, fewer problematic behaviors, higher student critical and creative thinking, greater participation and engagement, as well as increased motivation.[7] Use principles of learner-centered classrooms to convey love and belonging to your students.

One method for conveying your unconditional positive regard for students is by ending the day or class period with an optimistic closure.[8] We have developed ten prompts for you to close with, as an expression of appreciation for who they are as people. This will allow you to have two weeks' worth of unique prompts to choose from. Think of these as moments of gratitude. Over time, you may want to revise these so that students also consider something they saw or did for themselves and others.

Table 11.2 • Prompts for Communicating Positive Regard

Day 1	Something I appreciated about someone today was . . . because . . .
Day 2	I was really impressed by something I saw/heard today . . . because . . .
Day 3	I'm looking forward to tomorrow's class because . . .
Day 4	I really enjoyed when _____ said _____ because . . .
Day 5	I am very grateful that _____ was here in our class today because . . .
Day 6	I want to thank _____ because I got to learn about something new today.
Day 7	I appreciate how well we were able to _____ because . . .
Day 8	I saw how this class really pulled together to accomplish something hard when we . . .
Day 9	I felt successful today as a teacher because I was able to meet my goal of . . . I want to thank _____ for helping me achieve that when you . . .
Day 10	The collaborative groups we worked in today were amazing because . . .

TAKE ACTION

Exhibit optimism in your feedback. Optimism is a favorable view of students and what they can do in the future. Use what you have noticed in your strengths-spotting efforts, and tie that to your communication. For example, you might say, "I've noticed how determined you were when we were playing kickball. You can use that same determination when you're analyzing challenging texts."

Use voice feedback tools on student work. The growth of voice feedback tools, such as Google extensions like Kaizena and Mote, make it easy to give feedback on written work. Use tools like this so students can hear the sparkle in your voice, rather than read your words without context.

Use non-directivity to convey the regard you hold for learners. Hold individual conversations with students to help them identify their strengths, goals, and growth areas. Ask questions that mediate the student's thinking, rather than asking leading questions. Use shared decision-making about curriculum with students.

QUICK START

	I can start this tomorrow!	I can begin this month	I need to discuss this with others	Resources needed
Offer an optimistic closer each day to your students.				
Learn about voice feedback tools available at your school.				
Set up a schedule to meet with students individually for brief check-ins.				

IMMEDIACY

We hope you have all had an experience in which you felt close to a teacher. This closeness is known as *immediacy*. Dominique recalls a teacher from middle school who always seemed to know what to say to make people feel comfortable. The environment the teacher created was safe for learning, and the language, both verbal and nonverbal, was humane and growth producing. He came across as authentic (or, as Dominique would have said at the time, *real*). Students could relate to him. They thought of him as an ally and a mentor.

The concept of immediacy was introduced by social psychologist Albert Mehrabian, who noted that "people are drawn toward persons and things they like, evaluate highly, and prefer; and they avoid or move away from things they dislike, evaluate negatively, or do not prefer."[9] Mehrabian explained that humans engage in both approach and avoidance behaviors often based on the perceived distance between people. Education-specific implications of Mehrabian's principle of immediacy results in increased student motivation and the perception that what is being learned is relevant. Verbal and nonverbal cues in conveying value and importance, as well as connectiveness, to students signals immediacy and can improve learning outcomes.[10] Immediacy is part of teacher credibility. Combined with trust, competency, and dynamism, teacher credibility has an effect size of 1.09, which is a fairly powerful impact on learning.

Much of our communication is nonverbal, including eye contact, proximity, gestures, and touch. Consider the following examples of general things you can do to ensure that your students feel close to you:

- Gesture when talking to the class.

- Look at the class and smile while talking.

- Circulate around the room.

- Call students by name.
- Use "we" and "us" to refer to the class.
- Use vocal variety (pauses, inflections, stress, emphasis) when talking to the class.

To evaluate and increase your communication skills even further, you can use the Nonverbal Immediacy Self-Report Scale as a self-assessment to identify your potential areas of strength and growth opportunities.[11]

Figure 11.1 • Nonverbal Immediacy Self-Report Scale

Nonverbal Immediacy Self-Report Scale

Directions: The following statements describe the way some people behave while talking with or to others. Please indicate in the space at the left of each item the degree to which you believe the statement applies *to you.* Please use the following 5-point scale:

1 = Never; 2 = Rarely; 3 = Occasionally; 4 = Often; 5 = Very Often

_____ 1. I use my hands and arms to gesture while talking to people.

_____ 2. I touch others on the shoulder or arm while talking to them.

_____ 3. I use a monotone or dull voice while talking to people.

_____ 4. I look over or away from others while talking to them.

_____ 5. I move away from others when they touch me while we are talking.

_____ 6. I have a relaxed body position when I talk to people.

_____ 7. I frown while talking to people.

_____ 8. I avoid eye contact while talking to people.

_____ 9. I have a tense body position while talking to people.

_____ 10. I sit close or stand close to people while talking with them.

_____ 11. My voice is monotonous or dull when I talk to people.

_____ 12. I use a variety of vocal expressions when I talk to people.

_____ 13. I gesture when I talk to people.

_____ 14. I am animated when I talk to people.

_____ 15. I have a bland facial expression when I talk to people.

_____ 16. I move closer to people when I talk to them.

_____ 17. I look directly at people while talking to them.

(Continued)

(Continued)

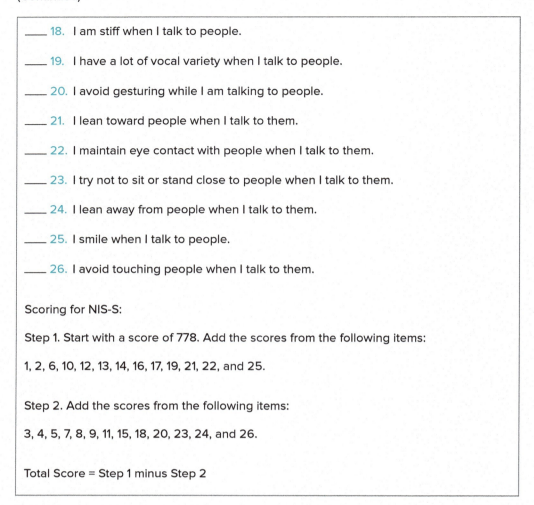

____ 18. I am stiff when I talk to people.

____ 19. I have a lot of vocal variety when I talk to people.

____ 20. I avoid gesturing while I am talking to people.

____ 21. I lean toward people when I talk to them.

____ 22. I maintain eye contact with people when I talk to them.

____ 23. I try not to sit or stand close to people when I talk to them.

____ 24. I lean away from people when I talk to them.

____ 25. I smile when I talk to people.

____ 26. I avoid touching people when I talk to them.

Scoring for NIS-S:

Step 1. Start with a score of 778. Add the scores from the following items:

1, 2, 6, 10, 12, 13, 14, 16, 17, 19, 21, 22, and 25.

Step 2. Add the scores from the following items:

3, 4, 5, 7, 8, 9, 11, 15, 18, 20, 23, 24, and 26.

Total Score = Step 1 minus Step 2

The tool provides a total score, and you can set personal goals to raise your score by increasing some behaviors and reducing others. Decide what you want to update in the classroom. Then, after you make the change, ask students or classroom visitors to use this scale to evaluate your nonverbal immediacy skills. This step will provide you with additional perspectives and allow you to fine-tune even further if desired.

TAKE ACTION

Get rid of physical barriers between yourself and your students. Sometimes desks get in the way. Sometimes it's the presentation equipment. Smartboards are a great innovation, but they can be misused if the teacher is always glued to the device. Pair your smartboard with a tablet so you can operate it from a distance This approach allows you to circulate and make regular contact with students.

The power of touch. We fully recognize that school systems have policies to ensure student safety, and these include physical contact with students. Of course, there are cultural and gender boundaries, too, and individuals have varying levels of tolerance for touch. But we are also social animals, and appropriate, consented touch can convey value and closeness. The relationships that develop when teachers can shake the hand of, fist bump, or elbow tap a student entering the room; place a hand on a student's shoulder to communicate that they are doing a great job; or high-five a student who has completed a major project can be amazing. In addition, it should be noted that teachers can "touch" with their eyes and words—a smile at the end of the presentation and the use of pronouns such as _we_ and _our_ all communicate value and respect.

Keep your immediacy appropriate and natural. Anything can be overdone, including immediacy. We're not looking for over-the-top performers or "phonies." Efforts to build immediacy need to be natural, not contrived. We've all been around a person whose eye contact makes us uncomfortable or a person whose gestures are a distraction. Don't let that become you, because your efforts to increase immediacy will not have the desired impact and may actually make things worse. It's also important to go slowly on this one. Your students are used to a certain style from you, and they value predictability. If you radically and swiftly change your style, they will notice. Take your time, and thoughtfully increase your immediacy with students.

QUICK START

	I can start this tomorrow!	I can begin this month	I need to discuss this with others	Resources needed
Scan your classroom to see if there is any furniture that is creating a visual barrier between you and your students.				
Record yourself teaching so you can watch for your use of supportive gestures and other nonverbal actions that demonstrate your immediacy.				
Complete the Nonverbal Immediacy Self-Report Scale to gauge your progress.				

TRUST

Students want to know that their teachers are trustworthy. Positive student-teacher relationships hold feelings of mutual trust at the center. Often, we only notice trust by its absence. "We inhabit a climate of trust as we inhabit an atmosphere and notice it as we notice air, only when it becomes scarce or polluted."[12] As educators, we need to ensure that trust is not scarce or polluted. Trust should be in the air, all around students, so that they can learn.

Strong student-teacher relationships rely on effective communication and a willingness to address issues that strain the relationship. Positive relationships are fostered and maintained when teachers set fair expectations, involve students in determining aspects of the classroom organization and management, and hold students accountable for the expectations in an equitable way.

Importantly, when classroom relationships between teachers and students are built on a foundation of trust, these relationships are not destroyed when students exhibit problematic behaviors. This is an important point for educators. If we want to ensure that students read, write, communicate, and think at high levels, then we have to develop positive, trusting relationships with *all* students.

Just as important, high levels of positive relationships build trust and make your classroom a safe place for students to explore what they do not know, including their errors and misconceptions. Indeed, powerful student-teacher relationships allow errors to be seen as opportunities to learn. A lot of students (and teachers) avoid situations where they are likely to make errors because they feel challenged by the thought of exposing their lack of knowledge or understanding. However, as educators we want to turn these situations into powerful learning opportunities, and this is more likely to occur in high-trust environments.

The Search Institute has created a Developmental Relationships Framework.[13] Their model has five major components expressed from the perspective of an individual student:

- Express care—show me that I matter to you.
- Challenge growth—push me to keep getting better.
- Provide support—help me complete tasks and achieve goals.
- Share power—treat me with respect and give me a say.
- Expand possibilities—connect me with people and places that broaden my world.

These components embody many of the dimensions of belonging discussed throughout this book. The following chart explores each dimension in more detail.

The Developmental Relationships Framework

Young people are more likely to grow up successfully when they experience developmental relationships with important people in their lives. Developmental relationships are close connections through which young people discover who they are, cultivate abilities to shape their own lives, and learn how to engage with and contribute to the world around them. Search Institute has identified five elements—expressed in twenty specific actions—that make relationships powerful in young people's lives.

Table 11.3 • The Developmental Relationships Framework

	Elements	Actions	Definitions
	Express Care Show me that I matter to you.	• **Be dependable**	Be someone I can trust.
		• **Listen**	Really pay attention when we are together.
		• **Believe in me**	Make me feel known and valued.
		• **Be warm**	Show me you enjoy being with me.
		• **Encourage**	Praise me for my efforts and achievements.
	Challenge Growth Push me to keep getting better.	• **Expect my best**	Expect me to live up to my potential.
		• **Stretch**	Push me to go further.
		• **Hold me accountable**	Insist I take responsibility for my actions.
		• **Reflect on failures**	Help me learn from mistakes and setbacks.
	Provide Support Help me complete tasks and achieve goals.	• **Navigate**	Guide me through hard situations and systems.
		• **Empower**	Build my confidence to take charge of my life.
		• **Advocate**	Stand up for me when I need it.
		• **Set boundaries**	Put limits in place that keep me on track.

	Elements	Actions	Definitions
	Share Power Treat me with respect and give me a say.	• **Respect me**.......................Take me seriously and treat me fairly. • **Include me**.......................Involve me in decisions that affect me. • **Collaborate**.......................Work with me to solve problems and reach goals. • **Let me lead**.......................Create opportunities for me to take action and lead.	
	Expand Possibilities Connect me with people and places that broaden my world.	• **Inspire**...............................Inspire me to see possibilities for my future. • **Broaden horizons**...........Expose me to new ideas, experiences, and places. • **Connect**............................Introduce me to people who can help me grow.	

Note: Relationships are, by definition, bidirectional, with each person giving and receiving. So each person in a strong relationship both engages in and experiences each of these actions. However, for the purpose of clarity, this framework is expressed from the perspective of one young person.

The Developmental Relationships Framework, copyright 2018, is used with permission from Search Institute, Minneapolis, MN USA, www.searchinstitute.org.

TAKE ACTION

Recognize that some students may not trust you or the content you teach.
There are students who come to the subject we teach with a level of mistrust of their own skills (e.g., "I've never been good at science") or because of past schooling experiences. Be patient with them as they build trust in themselves and in you. Prepare yourself for the fact that progress might not be seen for weeks or even months, but your persistence and faith in them will win them over.

Be prepared to repair trust when you are to blame. Teachers aren't perfect, and we make mistakes. At times, those mistakes may harm the relationship that we have with an individual student or even the entire class. When that happens, own up to it. There is a difference between impact and intent. Apologize, and resist the urge to make excuses. Make amends to regain trust with the young people involved. Be sure to forgive yourself too. Learn from your missteps and strive to avoid them in the future.

QUICK START[14]

	I can start this tomorrow!	I can begin this month	I need to discuss this with others	Resources needed
Stay in touch on the issues and concerns of your students.				
Anticipate and respond quickly to problems.				
Honor your commitments and keep promises.				

CASE IN POINT: WHEN UNCONDITIONAL POSITIVE REGARD IS CHALLENGED

Brenda Williams has taught middle school English in urban Title I schools for nearly fifteen years. Through experience, mistakes, and successes she has experienced firsthand the power of holding students to high academic standards, and she makes sure that students understand those expectations right from the start of every year. While her methods have pushed many students to work hard and achieve academic success over the years, inevitably (in her mind) some students have fallen through the cracks. Initially she worried about those students and tried to pull them along, but over time she developed this belief: *There isn't much I can do if students don't want to put in the effort to succeed.*

Toward the end of the previous school year, Ms. Williams began working with an instructional coach, who challenged her to reconsider the way in which she approached motivating her students toward success. Ms. Williams had been communicating the expectation that students had to earn her approval based on their behavior as well as their academic grades. But through discussion with the coach, she realized that this mindset was actually shutting students off from reaching their full potential and conveying unintended messages of unworthiness.

The instructional coach offered these suggestions:

- Rather than insult a student who is chronically late by using language such as, "Where have you been?" or "Glad you decided to show up," focus on welcoming the student with language such as, "So happy you're here today. Give me a minute, and I will catch you up to speed."

- Rather than making comments such as, "Your desk is a mess. You need to be more organized," focus on challenging students in a positive way, using language such as, "Staying organized helps us be prepared for learning. Let's figure out some ways that we can improve how you keep your desk."

Together Ms. Williams and the instructional coach developed a new mantra for her to keep in mind throughout the coming year: *Students deserve praise not based on their behavior or achievement but because of their right to be part of our class community and because of the positive contribution they can make just by being who they are.*

What's Your Advice?

- Ms. Williams is committed to being more intentional in communicating her unconditional positive regard to her students. What are three actions you would advise her to begin?

- How does the shift in mindset help Ms. Williams adopt a more unconditional positive regard for her students? How does this shift in mindset help students feel loved?

- Why might exclusively holding high academic achievement expectations not be enough for students to feel loved?

WHAT'S NEXT?

ESSENTIAL QUESTION

How do we love our students deeply and unconditionally?

THINK ABOUT

- How do your students know that you hold an unconditional positive regard for them?

- In what ways can you be intentional about your nonverbal signals of immediacy and closeness to your students?

- How are you building, maintaining, and repairing trust throughout the school year?

START – STOP – KEEP

Based on what you learned in this module, answer the questions that follow.

Start: What practice(s) would you like to start doing?

Stop: What practice(s) would you like to stop doing?

Keep: What practice(s) would you like to keep doing?

EPILOGUE

Where Do We Go From Here?

Now that we've unpacked each dimension individually, let's return to the big picture. At the beginning of the book, we defined belonging as "the feeling that we're part of a larger group that values, respects, and cares for us—and to which we feel we have something to contribute."[1] If we are part of a larger group, if that group values us, and if we can contribute, then we feel that we belong. If we are not part of a group, if we are not valued in the group, or if our contributions are not perceived as being useful, then we do not feel that we belong.

For example, just because we are part of a biological family, it does not guarantee that we experience belonging with those people. Just because we're good at mathematics, it does not mean that we feel a sense of belonging in the math club. And just because we have a certain level of income, it does not mean that we automatically feel belonging with our neighbors or professional colleagues. As educators, we need to keep these potential contradictions in mind as we focus on creating a sense of belonging in our schools.

There are at least eleven dimensions of belonging that educators can mobilize.[2] By attending to each of these, we can build a stronger sense of belonging for students. Each dimension has been the focus of a module in this book.[3]

Table E.1 · Fostering Dimensions of Belonging

Dimension	Essential Question	Actions We Could Take to Foster This Dimension at the Grade Level or School
Welcomed	How does the environment and various situations convey a consistent message of welcoming?	
Invited	How are we pursuing all students' presence and actively extending new invitations?	
Present	How do we ensure that all students are present for learning?	
Accepted	How are we receiving all learners unconditionally and graciously?	
Known	How do we get to know students personally and for the strengths they possess?	
Supported	How are we providing the assistance all students need to participate fully and meaningfully?	
Befriended	How are we creating opportunities for friendships to form and deepen?	
Involved	How do we engage students actively with, and alongside, peers in shared learning and common goals?	

Dimension	Essential Question	Actions We Could Take to Foster This Dimension at the Grade Level or School
Heard	How are we seeking out all learners' perspectives on issues that matter?	
Needed	How are we recognizing and receiving all our learners' talents, gifts, and contributions?	
Loved	How do we love our students deeply and unconditionally?	

While each dimension of belonging is unique and deserves specific attention, the dimensions are also highly interrelated. This means that as we focus on one dimension, we are often indirectly building up another. Consider these examples:

- When we **welcome** students by greeting them at the door, we are also showing them they are **known** when we use their name in the greeting, and we are indirectly affirming that their **presence** is valued.

- When we use class meetings to discuss academic or other important topics, we are allowing for students' voices to be **heard**, but we are also reaffirming that we want them **involved** in the discussion or problem-solving process and that their voice and perspective is valued and **needed** for the meeting to be successful.

- When we use text or instructional materials that reflect students' identities or lived experiences, we make them feel **known** and **accepted**. Using intentional grouping strategies for discussion and instruction also **invites** all students to the learning process and gives opportunities for **befriending** to take place within the class community.

- Let's look how one elementary school is working at creating a sense of belonging on their campus.

CASE IN POINT:
KERRYDALE ELEMENTARY SCHOOL, PRINCE WILLIAM COUNTY SCHOOLS (VIRGINIA)

The school staff at Kerrydale Elementary School has chosen to focus on belonging throughout this school year. They are a Visible Learning Certified school and have many processes and procedures in place that support students' learning. But Principal Alyse Zeffiro Kaptein wanted to take the students and staff to the next level. To begin, they used Hattie's effect size data to identify two aspects of belonging to build their teachers' strategic actions: strong classroom cohesion (effect size 0.66) and student-teacher relationships (effect size 0.62).

Figure E.1 · Effect Size of Strong Classroom Cohesion

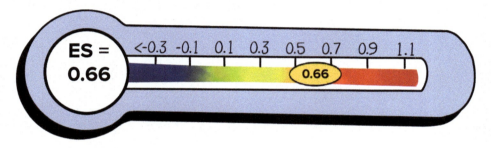

Figure E.2 · Effect Size of Student-Teacher Relationships

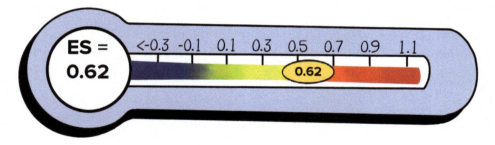

Figure E.3 · Effect Size of Belonging

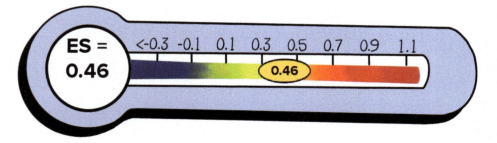

During their "welcome back" professional learning day, the staff engaged in two activities that helped them set the tone for the year. First, they engaged in a discussion about what it means to truly know a student and build a relationship with them. They determined that significant relationships weren't only about knowing a student's face and name—they also involved the following dimensions:

- knowing the learner's strengths,

- being familiar with their areas of growth,

- being able to talk about their likes and dislikes,

- knowing what is important to them, and

- knowing how they learn best.

To further visualize this concept, the principal set up a Dot Activity[4] by posting the new class rosters around the meeting room and giving teachers small dot stickers. During this activity, the teachers went around the room and placed a dot next to the name of the students they had a significant relationship with, based on the five factors identified in their discussion. When the teachers were finished, they examined each roster to see which students had dots and, importantly, which students did not.

The principal then presented the teachers with research explaining that when new students do not make a friend or do not have a significant relationship form within the first month of school, it negatively impacts their academic achievement and sense of belonging. The principal then gave each teacher their class roster and asked them to reflect on what specific actions they would take to ensure that all students had opportunities to build relationships and feel known, especially those learners without dots.

The teachers ended the day working in their grade-level teams to create grade-level norms focused on creating a strong sense of belonging for all students. Each grade-level team also committed to implementing targeted and intentional morning meetings that foster strong social cohesion. Here are some of the norms they created:

- Greet all students daily by name and find ways to celebrate students' uniqueness.

- Designate class ambassadors to welcome new students.

- Set intentional time each day for students to talk with peers.

- Continue to learn about and get to know students through the year, not just at the beginning.

- Make intentional opportunities for feedback—student to student, teacher to student, student to teacher, family/caregiver to teacher.

- Send weekly communication to families/caregivers to stay connected.

By the end of the day, the Kerrydale staff felt a sense of purpose, and the teachers were excited to have identified specific strategic actions they could implement to cultivate belonging from day 1 of the school year. As we've noted, a sense of belonging is their central tenet for the entire school year and should be revisited continually to ensure they are making learner-centered decisions. Several weeks into the school

(Continued)

(Continued)

year, Principal Alyse Zeffiro Kaptein shared the following story:

> We had one student in 4th grade who did not have any dots next to his name. He wasn't new to us; he was a child that teachers didn't forge relationships with. Well, the two 4th grade teachers took this information and made it a point to build a strong relationship with this student and he is shining! When you observe him in the classroom, he is a completely different child from the previous year, he is driving in his learning, asking questions, providing feedback, seeking and advocating for himself as a learner! When I asked him about this school year and how he was feeling, his response was: "This is the best year ever!" When I asked why, he said, "Because I know my teachers care about me and want me to learn and do my best." And when I asked if he felt he belongs in his classroom, he said, "Oh yea, we all do!" with a smile from ear to ear and a sense of pride!

Just like the teachers at Kerrydale, it's important for you to have a plan in place that you can use to strategically and intentionally cultivate belonging in your classroom. Regardless of whether you are working on this on your own, with a few colleagues, with your grade-level team, or with your entire school staff, here are some questions to help you build your plan:[5]

- What am I doing well right now?

- What should I be doing better or differently?

- What next steps should I take to strengthen this aspect of belonging?

Reflect on these questions for each dimension of belonging.

Now that you've reflected, analyze your notes. Are there any dimensions that stand out to you as being particularly strong in your classroom community? Are there any that are particularly weak? Which dimension(s) could you focus on to provide your classroom community with the greatest gains?

Make a plan to focus on one or two dimensions for the next two months. Go back to the module(s) and examine the Quick Start sections as well as the Take Action ideas. Use those prompts to decide on the concrete action steps that you will take as you focus on building that dimension in your classroom community.

"We all need to belong—somewhere and to someone."[6] Give your students the opportunity to belong in *your* classroom and *with you*.

END NOTES

INTRODUCTION

1. Cohen, G. L. (2022). *Belonging: The science of creating connection and bridging divides*. Norton.

2. Cai, Y., Yang, Y., Ge, Q., & Weng, H. (2022). The interplay between teacher empathy, students' sense of school belonging, and learning achievement. *European Journal of Psychology of Education*, *38*, 1167–1183. https://doi.org/10.1007/s10212-022-00637-6

3. Visible Learning Meta^XTM^. (n.d.). Corwin. www.visiblelearningmetax.com

4. Raufelder, D., Neumann, N., Domin, M., Lorenz, R. C., Gleich, T., Golde, S., Romund, L., Beck, A., & Hoferichter, F. (2021). Do belonging and social exclusion at school affect structural brain development during adolescence? *Child Development*, *92*(6), 2213–2223. https://doi.org/10.1111/cdev.13613

5. Walton, G. M., & Cohen, G. L. (2011). A brief social-belonging intervention improves academic and health outcomes of minority students. *Science*, *331*(6023), 1447–1451.

6. Boyd, D. T., Gale, A., Quinn, C. R., Mueller-Williams, A. C., Jones, K. V., Williams, E., & Lateef, H. A. (2023). Do we belong? Examining the associations between adolescents' perceptions of school belonging, teacher discrimination, peer prejudice and suicide. *Journal of Racial and Ethnic Health Disparities*. https://doi.org/10.1007/s40615-023-01622-5

7. Boyd, D. T., Gale, A., Quinn, C. R., Mueller-Williams, A. C., Jones, K. V., Williams, E., & Lateef, H. A. (2023). Do we belong? Examining the associations between adolescents' perceptions of school belonging, teacher discrimination, peer prejudice and suicide. *Journal of Racial and Ethnic Health Disparities*. https://doi.org/10.1007/s40615-023-01622-5

8. Vélez-Grau, C., & Lindsey, M. A. (2022). Do connectedness and self-esteem play a role in the transition to future suicide attempts among Latina and Latino youth with suicide ideation? *Children and Youth Services Review*, *139*, 106553.

9. Svetaz, M. V., Ireland, M., & Blum, R. (2000). Adolescents with learning disabilities: Risk and protective factors associated with emotional well-being: Findings from the National Longitudinal Study of Adolescent Health. *Journal of Adolescent Health*, *27*, 340–348.

OVERIEW

1. Adapted from: Carter, E. W. (2021). Dimensions of belonging for individuals with intellectual and developmental disabilities. In J. L. Jones & K. L. Gallus (Eds.), *Belonging and resilience in individuals with developmental disabilities* (pp. 13–33). Springer Nature.

2. Carter, E. W., & Biggs, E. E. (2021). *Creating communities of belonging for students with significant cognitive disabilities* (Belonging Series). University of Minnesota. TIES Center.

3. Jarmeka, L. M., Kane, H. S., & Bell, A. V. (2022). Threats to belonging and health: Understanding the COVID-19 pandemic using decades of research. *Social Issues and Policy Review, 16*(1), 125–163.

4. Allen, K., Kern, M. L., Rozek, C. S., McInereney, D., & Slavich, G. M. (2021). Belonging: A review of conceptual issues, an integrative framework, and directions for future research. *Australian Journal of Psychology, 73*(1), 87–102.

5. Lambert, N. M., Stillman, T. F., Hicks, J. A., Kamble, S., Baumeister, R. F., & Fincham, F. D. (2013). To belong is to—matter: Sense of belonging enhances meaning in life. *Personality and Social Psychology Bulletin, 39*(11), 1418–1427.

6. Cook, J. E., Purdie-Vaughns, V., & Cohen, G. L. (2012). Chronic threat and contingent belonging: Protective benefits of values affirmation on identity development. *Journal of Personality and Social Psychology, 102*(3), 479–496.

7. Murphy, M. C., & Zirkel, S. (2015). Race and belonging in school: How anticipated and experienced belonging affect choice, persistence, and performance. *Teachers College Record, 117*(12), 1–40.

8. Cemalcilar, Z. (2010). Schools as socialisation contexts: Understanding the impact of school climate factors on students sense of school belonging. *Applied Psychology, 59*(2), 243–272.

9. Schools for Health in Europe. (n.d.). *School physical environment.* https://www.schoolsforhealth.org/resources/glossary/school-physical-environment

10. Burgess, D. L., Kim, I., Seon, Y., & Chatters, S. J. (2023). Exploring dimensions of bias-based bullying victimization, school fairness, and school belonging through mediation analysis. *Psychology in the Schools, 60*(11), 4531–4544. https://doi.org/10.1002/pits.23015

11. García-Díaz, V., Urbano-Contreras, A., Iglesias-García, M. T., & Álvarez-Blanco, L. (2023). Identification, witnessing and reaction to school bullying behaviour in secondary education. *Child Indicators Research, 16*(4), 1627–1641.

12. SchoolSafety.gov. (2023). *Find resources to create a safer school.* www.schoolsafety.gov

13. Leithwood, K., & Janzti, D. (1999). The relative effects of principal and teacher sources of leadership on student engagement with school. *Educational Administration Quarterly, 35*(4), 679–706.

14. The Glossary of Education Reform. (2016, February 18). *Student engagement.* https://www.edglossary.org/student-engagement/

15. Akar-Vural, R., Yilmaz-Özelçi, S., Çengel, M., & Gömleksiz, M. (2013). The development of the "Sense of Belonging to School" scale. *Eurasian Journal of Educational Research*, *53*, 215–230.

16. TIMSS & PIRLS International Study Center. (2019). *School climate: Students' sense of school belonging*. https://timss2019.org/reports/students-sense-of-school-belonging/

17. Turnaround for Children Toolbox. (n.d.). *Measurement: Assess and reflect to become more attuned and responsive educators*. https://turnaroundusa.org/toolbox/measurement/well-beingindex/#automated

MODULE 1

1. Park, S., & Holloway, S. (2018). Parental involvement in adolescents' education: An examination of the interplay among school factors, parental role construction, and family income. *School Community Journal*, *28*(1), 9–36.

2. Murdoch, Y. D., Hyejung, L., & Kang, A. (2018). Learning students' given names benefits EMI classes. *English in Education*, *52*(3), 225–247.

3. Cook, C. R., Fiat, A., Larson, M., Daikos, C., Slemrod, T., Holland, E. A., Thayer, A. J., & Renshaw, T. (2018). Positive greetings at the door: Evaluation of a low-cost, high-yield proactive classroom management strategy. *Journal of Positive Behavior Interventions*, *20*(3), 149–159.

4. Allday, A., Bush, M., Ticknor, N., & Walker, L. (2011). Using teacher greetings to increase speed to task engagement. *Journal of Applied Behavior Analysis*, *44*, 393–396.

5. Alrubail, R. (2014). *Empathy & inclusion for ELL students*. Edutopia. http://www.edutopia.org/discussion/empathy-inclusion-ell-students

6. Lev, A. I., & Alie, L. (2012). *Improving emotional & behavioral outcomes for LGBT youth: A guide for professionals*. Paul H. Brookes.

7. Cook, C. R., Fiat, A., Larson, M., Daikos, C., Slemrod, T., Holland, E. A., Thayer, A. J., & Renshaw, T. (2018). Positive greetings at the door: Evaluation of a low-cost, high-yield proactive classroom management strategy. *Journal of Positive Behavior Interventions*, *20*(3), 149–159.

8. Tarr, P. (2004). Consider the walls. *Young Children*, *59*(3), 88–92.

9. American Psychological Association. (2018, April 19). *Power of the situation*. https://dictionary.apa.org/power-of-the-situation

10. Locke, C. (2023, April 25). *Diversity campus read author explains how 'situation-crafting' can combat racism*. UMass Chan Medical School. https://www.umassmed.edu/news/news-archives/2023/04/diversity-campus-read-author-explains-how-situation-crafting-can-combat-racism/

11. Cohen, J. L. (2022). *Belonging: The science of creating connection and bridging divides*. W. W. Norton.

12. Walton, G. M., & Cohen, J. L. (2011). A brief social-belonging intervention improves academic and health outcomes of minority students. *Science*, *331*(6023), 1447–1451.

MODULE 2

1. National Academies of Sciences, Engineering, and Medicine. (2020). *Social isolation and loneliness in older adults: Opportunities for the health care system*. The National Academies Press. https://doi.org/10.17226/25663

2. Raabe, I. J. (2019). Social exclusion and school achievement: Children of immigrants and children of natives in three European countries. *Child Indicators Research, 12*(3), 1003–1022.

3. Eisenberger, N. I., & Lieberman, M. D. (2004). Why rejection hurts: A common neural alarm system for physical and social pain. *Trends in Cognitive Science, 8*, 294–300. https://doi.org/10.1016/j.tics.,2004.05.010

4. Birch, S. H., & Ladd, G. W. (1997). The teacher-child relationship and children's early school adjustment. *Journal of School Psychology, 35*, 61–79.

5. TNTP. (2022). *Unlocking acceleration: How below-grade level work is holding students back in literacy*. https://tntp.org/assets/documents/Unlocking_Acceleration_8.16.22.pdf

6. Rosenshine, B. V. (2015). How time is spent in elementary classrooms. *Journal of Classroom Interaction, 50*(1), 41–53.

7. Purkey, W. W., & Novak, J. M. (1996). *Inviting school success: A self-concept approach to teaching, learning, and democratic practice* (3rd ed.). Wadsworth Publishing.

8. Ginsberg, M., & Wlodkowski, R. (2000). *Creating highly motivating classrooms for all students*. Jossey-Bass.

9. Fisher, D., & Frey, N. (2021). *Better learning through structured teaching* (3rd ed.). ASCD.

10. Rubie-Davies, C. (2014). *Becoming a high expectation teacher: Raising the bar*. Routledge.

11. Hattie, J. (2023). *Visible learning: The sequel: A synthesis of over 2,100 meta-analyses relating to achievement*. Routledge.

12. Recht, D. R., & Leslie, L. (1988). Effect of prior knowledge on good and poor readers' memory of text. *Journal of Educational Psychology, 80*(1), 16–20.

13. Price, H. E. (2021). The college preparatory pipeline: Disparate stages in academic opportunities. *American Educational Research Journal, 58*(4), 785–814.

14. Benner, A. D., Boyle, A. E., & Bakhtiari, F. (2017). Understanding students' transition to high school: Demographic variation and the role of supportive relationships. *Journal of Youth and Adolescence, 46*(10), 2129–2142.

MODULE 3

1. Attendance Works. (2022). *Why attendance matters for early childhood educators*. https://www.attendanceworks.org/wp-content/uploads/2019/06/Early-Childhood-Educators_May-2022_finalv2.pdf

2. United States Government Accountability Office. (2018, March). *K-12 education: Discipline disparities for black students, boys, and students with disabilities*. https://www.gao.gov/assets/gao-18-258.pdf

3. Losen, D. J., & Martinez, P. (2021). *Lost opportunities: How disparate school discipline continues to drive differences in the opportunity to learn.* Civil Rights Project. https://www.civilrightsproject.ucla.edu/research/k-12-education/school-discipline/lost-opportunities-how-disparate-school-discipline-continues-to-drive-differences-in-the-opportunity-to-learn/Lost-Opportunities_EXECUTIVE-SUMMARY_v17.pdf

4. United States Government Accountability Office. (2018, March). *K-12 education: Discipline disparities for black students, boys, and students with disabilities.* https://www.gao.gov/assets/gao-18-258.pdf

5. National Council on Disability. (2018). *The segregation of students with disabilities.* https://ncd.gov/sites/default/files/NCD_Segregation-SWD_508.pdf

6. Attendance Works. (2011). *Attendance in early elementary grades: Associations with student characteristics, school readiness, and third grade outcomes.* https://www.attendanceworks.org/wp-content/uploads/2017/06/ASR-Mini-Report-Attendance-Readiness-and-Third-Grade-Outcomes-7-8-11.pdf

7. Healthy Children. (2022, September 16). *School attendance, truancy & chronic absenteeism: What parents need to know.* American Academy of Pediatrics. https://www.healthychildren.org/English/ages-stages/gradeschool/school/Pages/School-Attendance-Truancy-Chronic-Absenteeism.aspx

8. Kirkpatrick, K. M. (2020). Adolescents with chronic medical conditions and high school completion: The importance of perceived school belonging. *Continuity in Education, 1*(1), 50–63.

9. Quaglia Institute. (n.d.). *Student voice: A decade of data.* https://quagliainstitute.org/uploads/originals/student-voice-grades-6-12-decade-of-data-report.pdf

10. Cribb Fabersunne, C., Lee, S. Y., McBride, D., Zahir, A., Gallegos-Castillo, A., LeWinn, K. Z., & Morris, M. D. (2023). Exclusionary school discipline and school achievement for middle and high school students, by race and ethnicity. *JAMA Network Open, 6*(10): e2338989. https://doi.org/10.1001/jamanetworkopen.2023.38989

11. Álvarez, B. (2021, September 10). *School suspensions do more harm than good.* National Education Association. https://www.nea.org/advocating-for-change/new-from-nea/school-suspensions-do-more-harm-good

12. Leung-Gagné, M., McCombs, J., Scott, C., & Losen, D. J. (2022). *Pushed out: Trends and disparities in out-of-school suspension.* Learning Policy Institute. https://doi.org/10.54300/235.277

13. Mendez, L. M. R., & Knoff, H. M. (2003). Who gets suspended from school and why: A demographic analysis of schools and disciplinary infractions in a large school district. *Education and Treatment of Children, 26*(1), 30–51.

14. Wang, R. (2022). The impact of suspension reforms on discipline outcomes: Evidence from California high schools. *AERA Open, 8.* https://doi.org/10.1177/23328584211068067

15. Thorsborne, M., & Vinegrad, D. (2004). *Restorative practice in schools: Rethinking behaviour management.* Inyahead Press.

16. US Department of Education. (2011). *Individuals with Disabilities Education Improvement Act of 2004.* https://sites.ed.gov/idea/regs/c

17. National Center for Education Statistics. (2023). Students with disabilities. *Condition of Education.* US Department of Education, Institute of Education Sciences. https://nces.ed.gov/programs/coe/indicator/cgg

MODULE 4

1. Abbott, L., & McGuinness, S. (2022). Change management in Northern Ireland's transformed integrated schools: "What we want is a school where you can be who you are and it's a safe place." *International Journal of Inclusive Education*, *26*(6), 576–591.

2. Centers for Disease Control and Prevention. (2018, August 7). *Adolescent and school health: Protective factors*. U.S. Department of Health and Human Services.

3. Klik, K. A., Cárdenas, D., & Reynolds, K. J. (2023). School climate, school identification and student outcomes: A longitudinal investigation of student well-being. *British Journal of Educational Psychology*, *93*(3), 806–824.

4. Parker, P. C., Perry, R. P., Chipperfield, J. G., Hamm, J. M., Daniels, L. M., & Dryden, R. P. (2022). Adjustment and acceptance beliefs in achievement settings: Implications for student wellbeing. *Social Psychology of Education, 25*(5), 1031–1049.

5. Resnick, M. D., Bearman, P. S., & Blum, R. W. (1997). Protecting adolescents from harm: Findings from the national longitudinal study on adolescent health. *Journal of the American Medical Association, 278*(10), 823–832.

6. Gowing, A. (2019). Peer-peer relationships: A key factor in enhancing school connectedness and belonging. *Educational & Child Psychology, 36*(2), 64–77.

7. Pettigrew, T. F., & Tropp, L. (2006). A meta-analytic test of intergroup contact theory. *Journal of Personality and Social Psychology, 90*(5), 751–783.

8. Makri-Botsari, E. (2015). Adolescents' unconditional acceptance by parents and teachers and educational outcomes: A structural model of gender differences. *Journal of Adolescence, 43*, 50–62.

9. Ryan, R., & Deci, E. (2000). Self-determination theory and the facilitation of intrinsic motivation, social development, and well-being. *American Psychologist, 55*(1), 68–78.

10. Driscoll, K. C., & Pianta, R. C. (2010). Banking time in head start: Early efficacy of an intervention designed to promote supportive teacher-child relationships. *Early Education & Development*, *21*(1), 38–64.

11. Brown, V. (2019). What we're reading. *Teaching Tolerance*, 62. https://www.learningforjustice.org/magazine/summer-2019/what-were-reading

12. Paris, D., & Alim, S. (2017). *Culturally sustaining pedagogies: Teaching and learning for justice in a changing world*. Teachers College Press.

13. Schroeder, M., Tourigny, E., Bird, S., Ottmann, J., Jeary, J., Mark, D., Kootenay, C., Graham, S., & McKeough, A. (2022). Supporting indigenous children's oral storytelling using a culturally referenced, developmentally based program. *The Australian Journal of Indigenous Education, 51*(2), 1–22. https://doi.org/10.55146/ajie.v51i2.50

14. Zapata, A., Valdez-Gainer, N., & Haworth, C. (2015). Bilingual picturebook making in the elementary school classroom. *Language Arts, 92*(5), 343–358.

15. Davis, J., & Allen, K. M. (2020). Culturally responsive mentoring and instruction for middle school black boys in STEM programs. *Journal of African American Males in Education, 11*(2), 43–58.

16. Kressler, B., Chapman, L. A., Kunkel, A., & Hovey, K. A. (2020). Culturally responsive data-based decision making in high school settings. *Intervention in School & Clinic*, *55*(4), 214–220.

17. Wheeler, R. S., & Swords, R. (2006). *Code-switching: Teaching standard English in urban classrooms* (p. xvii). National Council of Teachers of English.

18. Link, B. G., Struening, E. L., Neese-Todd, S., Asmussen, S., & Phelan, J. C. (2001). Stigma as a barrier to recovery: The consequences of stigma for the self-esteem of people with mental illnesses. *Psychiatric Services*, *52*(12), 1621–1626.

19. Flower, A., Burns, M. K., & Bottsford-Miller, N. A. (2007). Meta-analysis of disability simulation research. *Remedial & Special Education*, *28*(2), 72–79.

20. Lalvani, P., & Broderick, A. (2013). Institutionalized ableism and the misguided "Disability Awareness Day": Transformative pedagogies for teacher education. *Equity & Excellence in Education*, *46*(4), 468–483.

21. Centers for Disease Control and Prevention. (2023). *Youth risk behavior surveillance system: 2021 results*. https://www.cdc.gov/healthyyouth/data/yrbs/index.htm

22. Zhao, Y., Yang, L., Sahakian, B. J., Langley, C., Zhang, W., Kuo, K., Li, Z., Gan, Y., Li, Y., Zhao, Y., Yu, J., Feng, J., & Cheng, W. (2023). The brain structure, immunometabolic and genetic mechanisms underlying the association between lifestyle and depression. *Nature Mental Health*, *1*, 736–750. https://doi.org/10.1038/s44220-023-00120-1

23. Sheftall, A. H., Asti, L., Horowitz, L. M., Felts, A., Fontanella, C. A., Campo, J. V., & Bridge, J. A. (2016). Suicide in elementary school-aged children and early adolescents. *Pediatrics*, *138*(4), e20160436. https://doi.org/10.1542/peds.2016-0436

24. Centers for Disease Control and Prevention. (2023, May 8). *Facts about suicide*. https://www.cdc.gov/suicide/facts/index.htm

25. Northwestern Medicine. (2023, August). Warning signs of teen suicide. https://www.nm.org/healthbeat/healthy-tips/emotional-health/the-suicide-epidemic

MODULE 5

1. Purvanova, R. K. (2013). The role of feeling known for team member outcomes in project teams. *Small Group Research*, *44*(3), 298–331.

2. Seligman, M. E., Ernst, R. M., Gillham, J., Reivich, K., & Linkins, M. (2009). Positive education: Positive psychology and classroom interventions. *Oxford Review of Education*, *35*(3), 293–311.

3. Selig, M. (2016). *Changepower: 37 secrets to habit change success*. Routledge.

4. Meier, D. R. (2019). *Supporting literacies for children of color: A strength-based approach to pre-school literacy*. Routledge.

5. DeMink-Carthew, J., Netcoh, S., & Farber, K. (2020). Exploring the potential for students to develop self-awareness through personalized learning. *Journal of Educational Research*, *113*(3), 165–176.

6. Kavanagh, S. S. (2018). Practicing resistance: Teacher responses to intergroup aggression in the classroom. *Equity & Excellence in Education*, *51*(2), 146–160.

7. Galloway, R., Reynolds, B., & Williamson, J. (2020). Strengths-based teaching and learning approaches for children: Perceptions and practices. *Journal of Pedagogical Research*, *4*(1), 31–45.

8. Schutte, N. S., & Malouff, J. M. (2019). The impact of signature character strengths interventions: A meta-analysis. *Journal of Happiness Studies*, *20,* 1179–1196.

9. Butler-Barnes, S., Chavous, T., Hurd, N., & Varner, F. (2013). African American adolescents' academic persistence: A strengths-based approach. *Journal of Youth & Adolescence, 42*(9), 1443–1458.

10. Your Therapy Source. (2019, August 29). *Student strengths in the classroom: Find the positive.* https://www.yourtherapysource.com/blog1/2019/08/26/student-strengths-in-the-classroom-2/

11. Martin, A. J. (2006). Personal bests (PBs): A proposed multidimensional model and empirical analysis. *British Journal of Educational Psychology*, *76*(4), 803–825.

12. Martin, A. J. (2011). Personal best (PB) approaches to academic development: Implications for motivation and assessment. *Educational Practice and Theory*, *33,* 93–99.

13. Steele, C. M., & Aronson, J. (1995). Stereotype threat and the intellectual test performance of African Americans. *Journal of Personality and Social Psychology*, *69*, 797–811.

14. Spencer, S. J., Logel, C., & Davies, P. G. (2016). Stereotype threat. *Annual Review of Psychology*, *67*, 415–437.

15. Hattie, J. A. (2023). *Visible learning: The sequel. A synthesis of over 2,100 meta-analyses relating to achievement*. Routledge.

16. Dweck, C. S. (2006). *Mindset: The new psychology of success*. Ballantine.

17. Steele, D. M., & Cohn-Vargas, B. (2013). *Identity safe classrooms, grades K–5: Places to belong and learn*. Corwin.

18. American University School of Education. (2020, December 10). *How to foster a growth mindset in the classroom*. https://soeonline.american.edu/blog/growth-mindset-in-the-classroom/

MODULE 6

1. The Singju Post. (2016, February 27). *Brené Brown on listening to shame at TED Talk*. https://singjupost.com/brene-brown-on-listening-to-shame-at-ted-talk-full-transcript/?singlepage=1

2. Vygotsky, L. S. (1978). *Mind and society: The development of higher mental processes*. Harvard University Press.

3. Pyne, J., & Borman, G. D. (2020). Replicating a scalable intervention that helps students reappraise academic and social adversity during the transition to middle school. *Journal of Research on Educational Effectiveness*, *13*(4), 652–678.

4. Cole, S., Eisner, A., Gregory, M., & Ristuccia, J. (2013). *Helping traumatized children learn: Creating and advocating for trauma-sensitive schools* (Vol. 2). Massachusetts Advocates for Children, Trauma and Learning Policy Initiative.

5. Hattie, J. A. (2023). *Visible learning: The sequel: A synthesis of 2,100 meta-analyses related to achievement*. Routledge.

6. Frey, N., Fisher, D., & Almarode, J. (2023). *How scaffolding works: A playbook for supporting and releasing responsibility to students*. Corwin.

7. Minahan, J. (2019). Trauma-informed teaching strategies. *Educational Leadership*, *77*(2), 30–35.

8. Designs 4 Dignity. (n.d.). *Empowering lives through design*. https://www .designs4dignity.org/

9. Frey, N., Fisher, D., & Smith, D. (2020, October). Trauma-informed design in the classroom. *Educational Leadership*, *78*(2). https://www.ascd.org/el/articles/trauma-informed-design-in-the-classroom

10. Sherman, D. K., Lokhande, M., Müller, T., & Cohen, G. L. (2021). Self-affirmation intervention. In G. W. Walton & A. J. Crum (Eds.), *Handbook of wise interventions: How social psychology can help people change* (pp. 63–99). Guilford.

11. Steele, C. M. (1988). The psychology of self-affirmation: Sustaining the integrity of the self. In L. Berkowitz (Ed.), *Advances in experimental social psychology* (Vol. 21, pp. 261–302). Academic Press.

12. Cohen, G. L., Garcia, J., Purdie-Vaughns, V., Apfel, N., & Hrzustoski, P. (2009). Recursive processes in self-affirmation: Intervening to close the minority achievement gap. *Science*, *324*, 400–403.

13. Goyer, J. P., Garcia, J., Purdie-Vaughns, V., Binning, K. R., Cook, J. E., Reeves, S. L., Apfel, N., Taborsky-Barba, S., Sherman, D. K., & Cohen, G. L. (2017). Self-affirmation facilitates minority middle schoolers' progress along college trajectories. *Proceedings of the National Academy of Sciences - PNAS*, *114*(29), 7594–7599.

14. Cohen, G. L., & Sherman, D. K. (2014). Self-affirmation and social psychological intervention. *Annual Review of Psychology*, *65*, 333–371.

15. Cohen, G. L., & Sherman, D. K. (2014). Self-affirmation and social psychological intervention. *Annual Review of Psychology*, *65*, 333–371.

16. Manke, K. J., Brady, S. T., Baker, M. D., & Cohen, G. L. (2021). Affirmation on the go: A proof-of-concept for text message delivery of values affirmation in education. *Journal of Social Issues*, *77*(3), 888–910.

MODULE 7

1. Yust, P. K. S., Weeks, M. S., Williams, G. A., & Asher, S. R. (2023). Social relationship provisions and loneliness in school: Child- and classroom-level effects. *Journal of School Psychology*, *99*, 101218.

2. Ibid.

3. Ibid.

4. Tatum, B. D. (2017). *Why are all the Black kids sitting together in the cafeteria? And other conversations about race*. Basic Books.

5. Thompson, J., & Byrnes, D. (2011). A more diverse circle of friends. *Multicultural Perspectives, 13*(2), 93–99.

6. Tian, L., Huang, J., & Huebner, E. S. (2023). Profiles and transitions of cyberbullying perpetration and victimization from childhood to early adolescence: Multi-contextual risk and protective factors. *Journal of Youth & Adolescence, 52*(2), 434–448.

7. Walters, G. D., & Espelage, D. L. (2018). From victim to victimizer: Hostility, anger, and depression as mediators of the bullying victimization-bullying perpetration association. *Journal of School Psychology, 68*, 73–83.

8. Burr, J. A., Han, S. H., & Peng, C. (2020). Childhood friendship experiences and cognitive functioning in later life: The mediating roles of adult social disconnectedness and adult loneliness. Gerontologist, 60(8), 1456–1465.

9. Guralnick, M. J. (1992). A hierarchical model for understanding children's peer-related social competence. In S. L. Odom, S. R. McConnell, & M. A. McEvoy (Eds.), *Social competence of young children with disabilities* (pp. 37–64). Paul H. Brookes.

10. Parker, J. G., Rubin, K. H., Erath, S. A., Wojslawowicz, J. C., & Buskirk, A. A. (2006). Peer relationships, child development, and adjustment: A developmental psychopathology perspective. In D. Cicchetti & D. J. Cohen (Eds.), *Developmental psychopathology: Theory and method* (Vol. 2, 2nd ed., pp. 96–161). Wiley.

11. National Core Indicators. (2022). *2021–22 data at a glance.* Author. https://idd .nationalcoreindicators.org/wp-content/uploads/2023/05/0519_NCIIDD_ Visusummary-A.pdf

12. Paley, V. G. (1993). *You can't say you can't play.* Harvard University Press.

13. Chadsey, J., & Gun, H. K. (2005). Friendship facilitation strategies: What do students in middle school tell us? *Teaching Exceptional Children, 38*(2), 52–57.

14. Pearpoint, J., Forest, M., & Snow, J. (1992). *The inclusion papers: Strategies to make inclusion work.* Inclusion Press.

15. Hassani, S., Alves, S., Avramidis, E., & Schwab, S. (2022). The circle of friends intervention: A research synthesis. *European Journal of Special Needs Education, 37*(4), 535–553.

16. Smith, P. K., & Brain, P. (2000). Bullying in schools: Lessons from two decades of research. *Aggressive Behavior, 26*, 1–9.

17. National Center for Education Statistics. (2022). Bullying at school and electronic bullying. *Condition of Education.* US Department of Education, Institute of Education Sciences. https://nces.ed.gov/programs/coe/indicator/a10

18. National Center for Education Statistics. (2022). Bullying at school and electronic bullying. *Condition of Education.* US Department of Education, Institute of Education Sciences. https://nces.ed.gov/programs/coe/indicator/a10

19. National Center for Injury Prevention and Control. (2019). *Preventing bullying.* Centers for Disease Control and Prevention. https://www.cdc.gov/ violenceprevention/pdf/yv/bullying-factsheet508.pdf

20. Stop Bullying. (2021, May 21). *Effects of bullying.* https://www.stopbullying.gov/ bullying/effects

21. Stop Bullying. (2021, November 10). *Warning signs for bullying.* https://www .stopbullying.gov/bullying/warning-signs

22. National Center for Education Statistics. (2022). Students' reports of hate-related words and hate-related graffiti. *Condition of Education*. US Department of Education, Institute of Education Sciences. https://nces.ed.gov/programs/coe/indicator/a09

23. Stop Bullying. (2021, November 10). *Warning signs for bullying*. https://www .stopbullying.gov/bullying/warning-signs

24. Stop Bullying. (2021, November 10). *How to prevent bullying*. https://www .stopbullying.gov/prevention/how-to-prevent-bullying

25. Englander, E. K. (2017, Winter). Understanding bullying behavior: What educators should know and can do. *American Educator, 40*, 24–29.

MODULE 8

1. Chan, P., Graham-Day, K. J., Ressa, V., Peters, M. T., & Konrad, M. (2014). Beyond involvement: Promoting student ownership of learning in classrooms. *Intervention in School and Clinic, 50*(2), 105–113. https://doi.org/10.1177/1053451214536039

2. Wormington, S., & Linnenbrink-Garcia, L. (2017). A new look at multiple goal pursuit: The promise of a person-centered approach. *Educational Psychology Review, 29*(3), 407–445.

3. Hattie, J. A. (2023). *Visible learning: The sequel: A synthesis of 2,100 meta-analyses related to achievement*. Routledge.

4. Fisher, D., Frey, N., Amador, O., & Assof, J. (2018). *The teacher clarity playbook*. Corwin.

5. Bandura, A. (1977). Self-efficacy: Toward a unifying theory of behavioral change. *Psychological Review, 84*(2), 191.

6. Corwin Visible Learning Meta$^{x^-}$. (2023, June). *Self-efficacy*. https://www .visiblelearningmetax.com/influences/view/self-efficacy

7. Fisher, D., Frey, N., Ortega, S., & Hattie, J. (2023). *Teaching students to drive their learning: A playbook on engagement and self-regulation*. Corwin.

8. Adapted from Wabisabi Learning. (n.d.). *6 ways of building student confidence through your practice*. wabisabilearning.com/blogs/mindfulness-wellbeing/building-student-confidence-6-ways

9. Usable Knowledge. (2018). Building a culture of self-efficacy. *Harvard Graduate School of Education Blog*. https://www.gse.harvard.edu/ideas/usable-knowledge/18/09/building-culture-self-efficacy

10. Alter, P., & Haydon, T. (2017). Characteristics of effective classroom rules: A review of the literature. *Teacher Education & Special Education, 40*(2), 114–127.

11. Bailey, J. (2014). *Creating a classroom contract with students*. https://www .mainetoy.org/blog/post/creating-a-classroom-contract-with-students

12. Cascio, C. N., O'Donnell, M. B., Tinney, F. J., Lieberman, M. D., Taylor, S. E., Strecher, V. J., & Falk, E. B. (2016). Self-affirmation activates brain systems associated with self-related processing and reward and is reinforced by future orientation. *Social Cognitive and Affective Neuroscience, 11*(4), 621–629. https://doi.org/10.1093/scan/nsv136

13. Nordengren, C. (2022). *Step into student goal setting: A path to growth, motivation, and agency*. Corwin.

14. Almarode, J., Fisher, D., Thunder, K., & Frey, N. (2021). *The success criteria playbook: A hands-on guide to making learning visible*. Corwin.

15. Almarode, J., Fisher, D., Thunder, K., & Frey, N. (2021). *The success criteria playbook: A hands-on guide to making learning visible*. Corwin.

16. Usher, A., & Kober, N. (2012). *Student motivation: An overlooked piece of school reform*. Center for Education Policy.

17. Chan, P., Graham-Day, K. J., Ressa, V., Peters, M. T., & Konrad, M. (2014). Beyond involvement: Promoting student ownership of learning in classrooms. *Intervention in School and Clinic, 50*(2), 105–113. https://doi.org/10.1177/1053451214536039

18. Midwest Comprehensive Center. (2018). *Student goal setting: An evidence-based practice*. American Institutes for Research. https://www.air.org/sites/default/files/2021-06/MWCC-Student-Goal-Setting-Evidence-Based-Practice-Resource-508.pdf

MODULE 9

1. Quaglia, R. J., & Corso, M. J. (2014). *Student voice: The instrument of change*. Corwin.

2. Levin, B. (2000). Putting students at the centre in education reform. *International Journal of Educational Change, 1*(2), 155–172.

3. Fullan, M. G. (2001). *The new meaning of educational change* (3rd ed.). Teachers College Press.

4. Pandolpho, B. (2018). *Strategies to help your students feel heard*. Edutopia. https://www.edutopia.org/article/strategies-help-your-students-feel-heard/

5. Smith, D., Fisher, D., & Frey, N. (2022). *The restorative practices playbook*. Corwin.

6. Smith, D., Fisher, D., & Frey, N. (2022). *The restorative practices playbook*. Corwin.

7. Benner, M., Brown, C., & Jeffrey, A. (2019). *Elevating student voice in education*. Center for American Progress. https://www.americanprogress.org/article/elevating-student-voice-education/

8. Holquist, S. E., & Walls, J. (2021). "Not present in our ranks": Exploring equitable representation in student voice efforts for policy change. *Teachers College Record, 123*(8), 1–15.

9. Benner, M., Brown, C., & Jeffrey, A. (2019). *Elevating student voice in education*. Center for American Progress. https://www.americanprogress.org/article/elevating-student-voice-education/

10. Patrick, J. (2022). Student leadership and student government. *Research in Educational Administration & Leadership, 7*(1), 1–37.

11. Fletcher, A. (2005). *Meaningful student involvement: Guide to students as partners in school change*. SoundOut. https://soundout.org/2022/04/28/meaningful-student-involvement-guide-to-students-as-partners-in-school-change/

MODULE 10

1. Eisenberg, N., & Strayer, J. (1987). Critical issues in the study of empathy. In N. Eisenberg & J. Strayer (Eds.), *Empathy and its development* (pp. 1–13). Cambridge University Press.

2. Gini, G., Albiero, P., Benelli, B., & Altoe, G. (2007). Does empathy predict adolescents' bullying and defending behavior? *Aggressive Behavior*, *33*, 467–476. https://doi.org/10.1002/ab.20204

3. Egan, K. (1997). *The educated mind: How cognitive tools shape our understanding*. University of Chicago.

4. Fuligni, A. J., Smola, X. A., & Al Salek, S. (2022). Feeling needed and useful during the transition to young adulthood. *Journal of Research on Adolescence*, *32*(3), 1259–1266.

5. de Smedt, F., Van Keer, H., & Graham, S. (2019). The bright and dark side of writing motivation: Effects of explicit instruction and peer assistance. *Journal of Educational Research*, *112*(2), 152–167.

6. Braun, T., & von Oertzen, T. (2021). Empathy, cognitive functioning, and prosocial behavior in mentored children. *New Directions for Child & Adolescent Development*, *2021*(179), 41–57.

7. Deming, D. (2017). The growing importance of social skills. *The Quarterly Journal of Economics*, *132*(4), 1593–1640.

8. Sapon-Shevin, M. (1998). *Because we can change the world: A practical guide to building cooperative, inclusive classroom communities*. Allyn & Bacon.

9. Fisher, D., Frey, N., & Ahkavan, N. (2019). *This is balanced literacy: Increasing competence and confidence in reading and writing*. Corwin.

10. Dudley-Marling, C., & Murphy, S. (1997). A political critique of remedial reading programs: The example of reading recovery. *The Reading Teacher*, *50*, 460–468.

11. Kamil, M. L., Borman, G. D., Dole, J., Kral, C. C., Salinger, T., & Torgesen, J. (2008). *Improving adolescent literacy: Effective classroom and intervention practices* (NCEE #2008-4027). National Center for Education Evaluation and Regional Assistance, Institute of Education Sciences, US Department of Education. https://ies.ed.gov/ncee/WWC/Docs/PracticeGuide/adlit_pg_082608.pdf

12. Maheady, L., Harper, G. F., & Mallette, B. (2001). Peer-mediated instruction and interventions and students with mild disabilities. *Remedial and Special Education*, *22*, 4–15.

13. Fuchs, D., Fuchs, L., & Burish, P. (2000). Peer-assisted learning strategies: An evidence-based practice to promote reading achievement. *Learning Disabilities Research and Practice*, *15*(2), 85–91.

14. Alegre-Ansuategui, F. J., Moliner, L., Lorenzo, G., & Maroto, A. (2017). Peer tutoring and academic achievement in mathematics: A meta-analysis. *Eurasia Journal of Mathematics, Science and Technology Education*, *14*, 337–354.

15. Adapted from Mastropieri, M. A., & Scruggs, T. E. (2007). *The inclusive classroom: Strategies for effective instruction* (3rd ed., p. 183). Merrill/Prentice Hall. Copyright 2007 by Merrill/Prentice Hall. Reprinted with permission.

16. National Mentoring Resource Center. (2023). *Key topics*. https://nationalmentoring resourcecenter.org/research-tools/key-topics/

17. Karcher, M. J. (2005). Cross-age peer mentoring. In D. L. DuBois & M. J. Karcher (Eds.), *Handbook of youth mentoring* (pp. 266–285). Sage.

18. Dantzer, B., & Perry, N. (2023). Co-constructing knowledge with youth: What high-school aged mentors say and do to support their mentees' autonomy, belonging, and competence. *Educational Action Research*, *31*(2), 195–212.

19. McDaniel, S. C., & Besnoy, K. D. (2019). Cross-age peer mentoring for elementary students with behavioral and academic risk factors. *Preventing School Failure*, *63*(3), 254–258.

20. National Mentoring Resource Center. (2023). *Resources for mentoring programs*. https://nationalmentoringresourcecenter.org/resources-for-mentoring-programs/

21. National Mentoring Resource Center. (n.d.). https://nationalmentoring resourcecenter.org/

22. Mentoring Resource Center. (2008). *Building effective peer mentoring in schools: An introductory guide*. https://educationnorthwest.org/sites/default/files/building-effective-peer-mentoring-programs-intro-guide.pdf

MODULE 11

1. Noddings, N. (2015). *A richer, brighter future for American high schools*. Cambridge University Press.

2. Finley, L. J. (2003). How can I teach peace when the book only covers war? *OJPCR: The Online Journal of Peace and Conflict Resolution*, *5*(1), 150–165.

3. Haslip, M. J., Allen-Handy, A., & Donaldson, L. (2019). How do children and teachers demonstrate love, kindness, and forgiveness? Findings from an early childhood strength-spotting intervention. *Early Childhood Education Journal*, *47*, 531–547.

4. Liu, W. (2021). Does teacher immediacy affect students? A systematic review of the association between teacher verbal and non-verbal immediacy and student motivation. *Frontiers in Psychology*, *12*, 713978. https://doi.org/10.3389/fpsyg.2021.713978

5. Rogers, C. R. (1969). *Freedom to learn*. Charles E. Merrill.

6. McCombs, B. L., & Whisler, J. S. (1997). *The learner-centered classroom and school: Strategies for increasing student motivation and achievement*. Jossey-Bass.

7. Cornelius-White, J. (2007). Learner-centered teacher-student relationships are effective: A meta-analysis. *Review of Educational Research*, *77*(1), 113–143.

8. Aperture Education. (2019). *Ed-SERT special edition: Educator's guide to optimistic thinking*.

9. Mehrabian, A. (1971). *Silent messages*. Wadsworth.

10. Iaconelli, R., & Anderman, E. M. (2021). Classroom goal structures and communication style: The role of teacher immediacy and relevance-making in students' perceptions of the classroom. *Social Psychology of Education*, *24*(1), 37–58.

11. Development of the nonverbal immediacy scale (NIS): Measures of self- and other-perceived nonverbal immediacy. Eastern Communication Association, copyright © 1976 Eastern Communication Association, reprinted by permission of Informa UK Limited, trading as Taylor & Francis Group, www.tandfonline.com on behalf of 1976 Eastern Communication Association.

12. Baier, A. (1994). Trust and antitrust. *Ethics*, *96*, 231–260.

13. The Search Institute. (2018). *The developmental relationships framework*. https://www.search-institute.org/developmental-relationships/developmental-relationships-framework/

14. Zenger, J., & Folkman, J. (2019, February 5). *The 3 elements of trust*. Harvard Business Review. https://hbr.org/2019/02/the-3-elements-of-trust

EPILOGUE

1. Cohen, G. L. (2022). *Belonging: The science of creating connection and bridging divides*. W. W. Norton.

2. Carter, E. W. (2021). Dimensions of belonging for individuals with intellectual and developmental disabilities. In J. L. Jones & K. L. Gallus (Eds.), *Belonging and resilience in individuals with developmental disabilities* (pp. 13–33). Springer Nature. https://doi.org/10.1007/978-3-030-81277-5_2

3. Carter, E. W. (2021). Dimensions of belonging for individuals with intellectual and developmental disabilities. In J. L. Jones & K. L. Gallus (Eds.), *Belonging and resilience in individuals with developmental disabilities* (pp. 13–33). Springer Nature. https://doi.org/10.1007/978-3-030-81277-5_2

4. Smith, D., Fisher, D., & Frey, N. (2021). *Removing labels, K–12: 40 techniques to disrupt negative expectation about students and schools*. Corwin.

5. Carter, E. W. (2021). Dimensions of belonging for individuals with intellectual and developmental disabilities. In J. L. Jones & K. L. Gallus (Eds.), *Belonging and resilience in individuals with developmental disabilities* (pp. 13–33). Springer Nature. https://doi.org/10.1007/978-3-030-81277-5_2

6. Carter, E. W. (2021). Dimensions of belonging for individuals with intellectual and developmental disabilities. In J. L. Jones & K. L. Gallus (Eds.), *Belonging and resilience in individuals with developmental disabilities* (pp. 13–33). Springer Nature. https://doi.org/10.1007/978-3-030-81277-5_2

INDEX

A Sage Company

CORWIN HAS ONE MISSION: to enhance education through intentional professional learning.

We build long-term relationships with our authors, educators, clients, and associations who partner with us to develop and continuously improve the best evidence-based practices that establish and support lifelong learning.

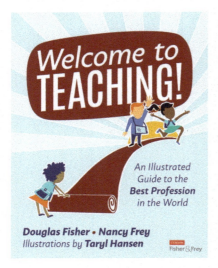
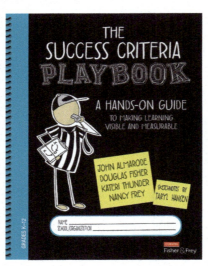
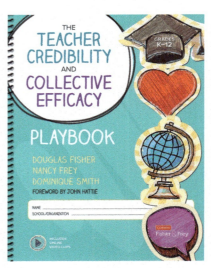
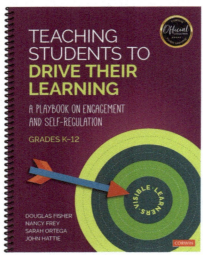
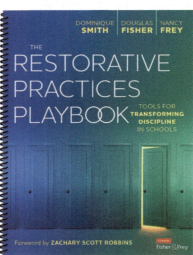
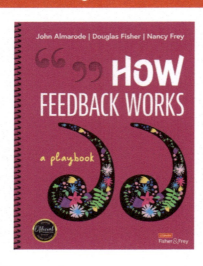
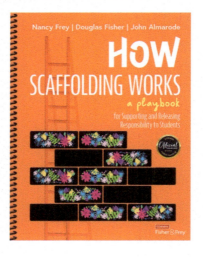
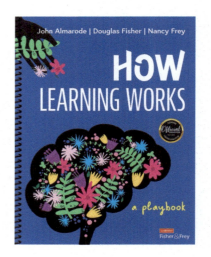

Put your learning into practice

When you're ready to take your learning deeper, begin your journey with our PD services. Our personalized professional learning workshops are designed for schools or districts who want to engage in high-quality PD with a certified consultant, measure their progress, and evaluate their impact on student learning.

CORWIN Teacher Clarity

Students learn more when expectations are clear

As both a method and a mindset, Teacher Clarity allows the classroom to transform into a place where teaching is made clear. Learn how to explicitly communicate to students what they will be learning on a given day, why they're learning it, and how to know if they were successful.

Get started at corwin.com/teacherclarity

CORWIN PLC+

Empower teacher teams to build collective agency and remove learning barriers

It's not enough to just build teacher agency, we must also focus on the power of the collective. Empowering your PLCs is a step toward becoming better equipped educators with greater credibility to foster successful learners.

Get started at corwin.com/plc

CORWIN Visible Learning+®

Translate the science of how we learn into practices for the classroom

Discover how learning works and how this translates into potential for enhancing and accelerating learning. Learn how to develop a shared language of learning and implement the science of learning in schools and classrooms.

Get started at corwin.com/visiblelearning

Experience the Corwin Difference.
Learn more at **corwin.com/the-corwin-difference**

FF23810050

NOTES

NOTES

NOTES

NOTES

NOTES